The New

Enchantment of America

TENNESSEE

By Allan Carpenter

CHILDRENS PRESS, CHICAGO

ACKNOWLEDGMENTS

For assistance in the preparation of the revised edition, the author thanks:
ROBIN MC CORD of the Tennessee Department of Tourist Development.

American Airlines—Anne Vitaliano, Director of Public Relations; *Capitol Historical Society,*
Washington, D.C.; *Newberry Library,* Chicago, Dr. Lawrence Towner, Director; *North-
western University Library,* Evanston, Illinois; *United Airlines*—John P. Grember, Manager
of Special Promotions; Joseph P. Hopkins, Manager, News Bureau.

UNITED STATES GOVERNMENT AGENCIES: *Department of Agriculture*—Robert Hailstock, Jr.,
Photography Division, Office of Communication; Donald C. Schuhart, Information Divi-
sion, Soil Conservation Service. *Army*—Doran Topolosky, Public Affairs Office, Chief of
Engineers, Corps of Engineers. *Department of Interior*—Louis Churchville, Director of
Communications; EROS Space Program—Phillis Wiepking, Community Affairs; Charles
Withington, Geologist; Mrs. Ruth Herbert, Information Specialist; Bureau of Reclama-
tion; National Park Service—Fred Bell and the individual sites; Fish and Wildlife Service—
Bob Hines, Public Affairs Office. *Library of Congress*—Dr. Alan Fern, Director of the
Department of Research; Sara Wallace, Director of Publications; Dr. Walter W. Ristow,
Chief, Geography and Map Division; Herbert Sandborn, Exhibits Officer. *National
Archives*—Dr. James B. Rhoads, Archivist of the United States; Albert Meisel, Assistant
Archivist for Educational Programs; David Eggenberger, Publications Director; Bill Leary,
Still Picture Reference; James Moore, Audio-Visual Archives. *United States Postal Serv-
ice*—Herb Harris, Stamps Division.

For assistance in the preparation of the first edition, the author thanks:
Mr. R.R. Vance, former Consultant, Division of Instruction, State of Tennessee, Depart-
ment of Education; Buford Ellington, former Governor; Earl L. Shaub, Director, Division
of Information and Tourist Promotion; Charles C. Sorsby, Supervisor of Economic
Research, Division of Economic Development; Tennessee Historical Commission;
Greater Knoxville Chamber of Commerce; Memphis Area Chamber of Commerce.

Illustrations on the preceding pages:
Cover photograph: Great Smoky
Mountains National Park, Jim Rowan
Page 1: Commemorative stamps of historic
interest
Pages 2-3: Bloody Pond, Fall Colors, USDI,
NPS, Shiloh National Military Park
Page 3 (Map): USDI Geological Survey
Pages 4-5: Memphis area, EROS Space
Photo, USDI Geological Survey, EROS
Data Center

Project Editor, Revised Edition:
  Joan Downing
Assistant Editor, Revised Edition:
  Mary Reidy

**Library of Congress Cataloging in
Publication Data**

Carpenter, John Allan, 1917-
  Tennessee.

  (His The new enchantment of America)
  SUMMARY: Discusses the history,
geography, resources, and sites of interest
in Tennessee and describes the
achievements of many famous
Tennesseans.
  1. Tennessee—Juvenile Literature.
[1. Tennessee] I. Title. II. Series.
F436.3.C3. 1979   976.8   78-11522
ISBN 0-516-04142-8

Contents

A True Story to Set the Scene

It was December 16, 1811, a day that struck awe into the hearts of the Chickasaw Indians. Almost fifteen thousand acres (six thousand hectares) of their hunting grounds in northwest Tennessee disappeared.

The sun was blotted out. Daylight turned to darkness. The earth trembled, the land dropped, and the Mississippi River swept in. The Chickasaw's hunting grounds lay at the bottom of what is now Reelfoot Lake.

The lake was created by an earthquake, but it took its name from an Indian legend.

A brave who walked awkwardly because of a club foot was named Kalopin, or Reelfoot. He could not persuade any girl of his tribe to marry him. Desperate, he went to visit the Choctaw and found a beautiful girl, Laughing Eyes. But her father smashed the peace pipe to the ground when Reelfoot asked him to approve the marriage.

Reelfoot had decided to kidnap his beloved. Then he dreamed that if he did so, the earth would quake and engulf his own village. He went away without his bride but later changed his mind and carried her off. As the drums beat out the wedding rhythms, the earth began to sway. The ground suddenly opened up, the Mississippi rushed in, and, according to the story, Reelfoot and his bride were swallowed by the lake that now carries his name.

Today Reelfoot Lake still serves as a reminder of Tennessee's legendary past and the beauty and resources of the present.

Reelfoot Lake (opposite), created by an 1811 earthquake, has one of the most abundant fish populations in the world.

Lay of the Land

THREE FOR THE PRICE OF ONE

"In Tennessee you get three states for the price of one," an observer commented on the three very distinct sections of Tennessee. East Tennessee is a region of high mountains, large lakes, and fertile valleys, where wilderness areas still look much as they did in the days of Daniel Boone. Middle Tennessee is a land of beautiful farms, and in West Tennessee are the rich plains of the Mississippi River.

Tennessee is further subdivided into eight physiographic regions. These are the Unaka Mountains (including the Great Smoky Mountains), the Great Valley of East Tennessee, the Cumberland Plateau and Mountains, the Highland Rim, the Central Basin, the Western Valley of the Tennessee River, the Mississippi Plateau, and the Mississippi Alluvial Plain.

The largest of these is the Highland Rim, covering 12,650 square miles (32,763 square kilometers). It completely encircles the Central Basin, somewhat like the rim of a saucer.

No state has more neighbor states than Tennessee, and only one other state—Missouri—has as many, eight in all. Tennessee is bordered by Kentucky and Virginia to the north; North Carolina on the east; Georgia, Alabama, and Mississippi on the south; and Arkansas and Missouri on the west.

The state's main natural boundaries are the Mississippi River on the west and the 70 miles (112 kilometers) of jagged border between Tennessee and North Carolina that follows the crest of the Smoky Mountains.

The origin of the name Tennessee is really unknown. It probably came from the Indian village named Tanasi, which stood on the Little Tennessee River. No one knows what the word originally meant in the Indian language.

Opposite: There are over 900 square miles (over 2,331 square kilometers) of inland water in Tennessee.

PHYSICAL FEATURES

Tennessee lies within three main river drainage systems—the Tennessee, Cumberland, and Mississippi. The Tennessee and Cumberland both eventually empty into the Mississippi. Several small streams flow across the state and empty directly into the Mississippi. These include the Obion, Forked Deer, Hatchie, Wolf, and Loosahatchie rivers.

The Tennessee River is formed about four miles (six kilometers) to the east of Knoxville's business district, where the French Broad and Holston rivers meet. The Tennessee flows to the south and west until it leaves Tennessee; then it does an about-face at the border between Mississippi and Alabama. There it turns back into Tennessee and flows north across the state to the Kentucky border. The Tennessee River drains more than half the state, with such tributaries as the Clinch, Hiwassee, Little Tennessee, Duck, and Elk.

The Cumberland River is joined by the Red, Harpeth, Stones, Obey, and other rivers.

The twenty-two major lakes of Tennessee are known as the Great Lakes of the South. Most of these are man-made, and their waters lap at 10,000 miles (16,000 kilometers) of shoreline.

The lakes of East Tennessee dot numerous valleys encompassed by majestic mountains; they include Boone, Calderwood, Cherokee, Chickamauga, Chilhowee, Douglas, Fort Patrick Henry, Fort Loudoun, Norris, Ococee, South Holston, Watauga, and Watts Bar.

With the exception of Woods Reservoir, the clear, freshwater lakes of Middle Tennessse were built by the United States Corps of Engineers. Others are the Center Hill, Cheatham, Dale Hollow, Great Falls, and Old Hickory. West Tennessee's major lakes are Kentucky, Pickwick, and Reelfoot.

If Tennessee is protected by a "moat" (the Mississippi) on the west, it is shielded on the east by a "great wall"—the Great Smoky Mountains, covering about 2,620 square miles (6,812 square kilometers) in Tennessee.

The Valley of the Tennessee nestles at the base of the Smokies, covering 7,450 square miles (19,370 square kilometers) and averag-

12

*Fall Creek Falls
State Park and Forest,
near Pikeville.*

ing 45 miles (72 kilometers) in width. It is formed by the Tennessee River and its tributaries.

To the west of the Valley are the Cumberland Plateau and Mountains, spreading more than 4,300 square miles (11,137 square kilometers) and rising to heights of 3,500 feet (1,050 meters) in the mountain sections. The plateau is about 60 miles (96 kilometers) wide at the northern border, narrowing to approximately 30 miles (48 kilometers) at the southern border.

IN ANCIENT TIMES

Fossils of snails, fish, molluscs, sea urchins, and other sea creatures indicate that at one time shallow seas covered most of what is now Tennessee. At intervals the land rose, was worn away, and rose again. The Appalachian Mountains were preceded by a range known as the Ancestral Appalachians. The present mountains probably at one time were almost twice as high as they are now. Because they are

13

such old mountains, they have weathered and worn considerably.

The Grand Canyon of the Tennessee, not far from Chattanooga, has been described as one of the geological wonders of the Western Hemisphere. It may have been carved out by the river over a period as long as seventy million years.

The mammoth ice masses that swept North America during the four glacial ages did not reach into what is now Tennessee; however, they had a great effect on the area. The prehistoric seas and later the ice ages drove animals and birds into the Cumberland region at times when plant and animal life elsewhere were destroyed. When the seas and the glaciers went their way, the plant and animal forms that had been preserved in the shelter of the Cumberlands gradually spread out to other regions, returning them to life.

Almost every force of nature has been at work in what is now Tennessee—even volcanoes. Volcanic rock is found in the Norris Basin, while volcanic ash up to three feet (one meter) thick covers some areas of **Middle** Tennessee. Forces of nature continue to change the face of Tennessee today.

CLIMATE

Average rainfall in Tennessee varies from 40 to 50 inches (101 to 127 centimeters) a year. There are usually no serious droughts or prolonged rainy spells. Only about 110 days of the 365 are entirely cloudy. Winds moving through the long valleys tend to keep the climate moderate both in winter and in summer, and the ranges of hills protect much of the state from most of the violent windstorms that otherwise might strike. Even the coldest periods of winter, with "severe" spells down to 15 to 20 degrees above zero Fahrenheit (minus 9.4 to 6.7 degrees Celsius), are generally relieved by thaws and mild weather. The eastern mountainous area enjoys moderately warm summer days, with cool nights. In other parts of the state some sultry weather occurs, but it usually is not too severe or long lasting.

The growing season ranges from 150 to 210 days in the east and from 180 to 230 days in the west.

Footsteps on the Land

PREHISTORIC PEOPLES

Their beautiful pottery lay just where they had left it. A shiny black finish still covered the hard clay floors. Apparently they quite suddenly left their homes and everything in them. Who were the people of this prehistoric village near Nashville? What happened to them? No one knows for certain. However, this ancient fortified town, once protected by wooden watchtowers, is only one of the many reminders of the people who have occupied the Tennessee region for many thousands of years.

Even more mysterious is the Old Stone Fort, near Manchester. Its earth walls are twenty feet (six meters) thick, faced on both sides with skillfully laid stonework. Inside are defenses that experts say could have been made only by experienced engineers. Many feel that the fort must have been made by the earliest European explorers. Other authorities assert that it was constructed by native Americans.

Another prehistoric fortified city, near Henderson, is named Cisco Village for J.G. Cisco, who excavated much of the site. There are thirty-five mounds, which were used for defense and other purposes. A pyramid-shaped base mound seems to have served as a temple.

Among the largest of the pyramid mounds is one of the Pinson mounds in Madison County. This one rises about seventy feet (twenty-one meters). Other large mounds include the Great Mound Group of Cheatham County.

The earliest prehistoric people of Tennessee were probably cave dwellers. Along the Wolf and Obey rivers, some traces have been found of people who lived on cliffs, much as the cliff dwellers of New Mexico and Arizona did.

Later people built houses like those found in the Humphreys County mound group. They were circular, 20 to 30 feet (6 to 9 meters) across. Dirt was banked up about 2 feet (.6 meter) around the base of each house. Posts driven into the dirt supported the walls

Chucalissa Prehistoric Indian Town, near Memphis, has been restored to look much as it did when the Yuchi lived there.

and roof of thatch. A small opening in the side served as a door, and a hole in the roof let out the smoke. The clay floors were smoothed and pressed firm by many feet.

The first peoples probably had to live by hunting. Gradually they began to cultivate crops and finally based their culture on the growing of maize, the Indian corn. Baskets of corn were often buried with the dead; many of these baskets have been found, still fairly well preserved.

Later the people learned to make pottery. Many terra-cotta pieces have been found, baked in the shape of animals or humans. Other objects were carved from stone. A smoking pipe found at Dill Branch at Shiloh has been described by one archaeologist as "the most perfect piece of prehistoric carving."

The earlier people buried their dead in caves; later, many dead were buried in vaults made of neatly cut stone slabs.

Among other important prehistoric Tennessee sites are the mounds on Chickamauga Creek and De Graffenreid Works, near Franklin.

A more recent people were the Yuchi, who lived along the Little Tennessee River. Several hundred years before the arrival of Europeans, there was a string of Yuchi villages along the east shore of the Mississippi River. One of the best known of these is Chucalissa Prehistoric Indian Town, near Memphis. It has been restored to look much as it did when the Yuchi called it home.

WAITING FOR CIVILIZATION

Two major Indian groups occupied Tennessee at the beginning of historic times. The mighty Iroquois nation was represented by the Cherokee. Legends told of their coming into the region from earlier homes near Lake Erie. They took over much of what is now East and Middle Tennessee and lived there for generations.

The other major group in the area, the Chickasaw, was a branch of the Muskhogean nation. The Chickasaw were among the smaller tribes of the South, but they were strong fighters and held their own against all comers. They held sway in West Tennessee.

Although they spoke different languages and belonged to different nations, the Cherokee and Chickasaw had many things in common. They lived in villages and cultivated vegetable and tobacco gardens. Corn was so important in their lives that they held an annual green-corn dance. Nuts, berries, and the abundant wild game and fish kept them well supplied with food.

They lived in permanent houses supported by heavy posts with smaller posts set between. Wood splints or twigs were woven through the upright posts, and these woven walls were covered with clay. Beneath the smoke hole was a raised place for the fire.

Clothing included fur robes, skin shirts, and leather leggings with fringe. Robes were made of feathers or woven of fiber or buffalo hair. Women wore short, shirtlike dresses made of deerskin; in colder weather they wrapped themselves in fur stoles. Much of the clothing was dyed or decorated with bright red and black.

Henry Timberlake described the Cherokee: "Of middle stature, of an olive color, tho' generally painted, and their skins stained with gunpowder, pricked into very pretty figures. The hair of their head is shaved, tho' many of the old people have it plucked out by the roots, except a patch on the hinder part of the head, about twice the bigness of a crownpiece, which is ornamented with beads, feathers, wampum, stained deer's hair, and such like baubles.''

The Cherokee had a reputation for being very democratic. The women had their own organization—a council made up of the head women from each family clan. At the head of this group was the women's leader, known as the Beloved Woman of the Nation.

The Shawnee, a wandering group of the Algonquin nation, were latecomers to the region. One of their villages stood at the present site of Nashville. They were resented by both the Cherokee and Chickasaw. The latter tribes were able to drive the Shawnee out of Tennessee in 1714.

At one time or another, other smaller Indian groups, such as the Chisca, also lived in Tennessee.

This diorama depicts
Tennessee Indian life.

BEGINNINGS

The first European known to have touched Tennessee was Hernando De Soto. In April, 1541, after wandering over much of the southeastern part of the United States, De Soto and his little army reached the bluffs of Memphis. Perhaps they had their first glimpse of the Mississippi River. With great ceremony, they planted the Spanish flag and took possession of the region in the name of their king. Some historians say that De Soto visited other parts of what is now Tennessee, but others agree that he and his party probably never touched more than the southwestern corner.

More than a hundred years passed before other Europeans came. Explorers Father Jacques Marquette and Louis Jolliet glided down the Mississippi River in 1673. Below the bluffs of modern Memphis, they were graciously greeted by the Chickasaw. In that same year James Needham and his servant, Gabriel Arthur, crossed the mountains and explored East Tennessee. They had been sent by Virginia trader Abraham Wood to investigate the possibility of trade with the Overhill Cherokee—those who lived to the west of the mountains.

Probably other Europeans visited the Tennessee region, but little is known about them. The next visitor of record was Robert Cavelier, Sieur de La Salle, who came down the Mississippi in 1682. When Pierre Prudhomme, a member of the La Salle party, was lost on a hunting trip, La Salle became alarmed and built a fort near Henning. Prudhomme eventually was found; he and a few men stayed at Fort Prudhomme, named after him, while La Salle went on down the river.

CONTINUINGS

By the 1680s three nations formally claimed the region that now contains Tennessee. The Spanish based their claim on the visit of De Soto. French claims were made by Marquette and Jolliet and La Salle. The British colonies on the coast contended that their charters extended at least to the Mississippi River, if not to the Pacific coast. As early as 1663 Tennessee was considered a part of the Carolinas. When North and South Carolina separated in 1693, Tennessee technically became a part of North Carolina.

After Needham's and Arthur's visit, English traders and trappers hurried across the mountains into the region. Soon the Indians had European guns, pans, blankets, and other items, for which they traded beaver and deer skins as well as products needed by the Europeans. Traders established themselves at the Indian villages, where they lived in relative luxury. They frequently gained favor with the Indians by marrying into the tribe.

Other Europeans in the country were hunters and trappers, generally known as Long Hunters because of the long periods when they would have to be gone from their homes.

In 1730 Sir Alexander Cuming went into the Cherokee country and befriended them. He told the Indians of the great king across the sea; they signed a treaty and even consented to be subjects of the king of England. When Cuming returned to England, he took several braves with him, including one who later became the most famous Indian leader of the region—Attakullakulla (Little Carpenter). The king treated them royally, and they came home to tell of the wonders they had seen in London.

The Chickasaw were even more friendly to the English. In fact, they later claimed that they had never lifted a war axe against the English people. The French were determined to destroy the Chickasaw allies of the English. They built Fort Assumption in 1740 to keep the Chickasaw from attacking their boats on the Mississippi, but the Chickasaw continued to rule the region. When war broke out between France and England in 1754, the French did all they could to turn the Cherokee against the English. To protect the frontier, the British, through the efforts of the governor of South Carolina, built Fort Loudoun—the first English structure in the Tennessee Valley. This fort, five miles (eight kilometers) west of the Cherokee capital of Echota, near present Knoxville, was completed in 1757.

Relations between the Cherokee and the colonies on the coast worsened, despite the efforts of chiefs Old Hop and Attakullakulla.

20

Murals in the Tennessee state capitol, Nashville, depict historical times.

By early 1760 the whole Cherokee nation, except for Attakullakulla, was at war with the English. The Indians laid siege to Fort Loudoun and starved the garrison into surrender after months of hardship.

British soldiers and colonial militia moved into the area, and on November 9, 1761, the Cherokee signed a treaty of peace and returned Fort Loudoun. In 1763 the French gave up all of their claims in North America.

In that same year, the English king issued a proclamation forbidding European settlement west of the mountains. Land-hungry settlers disregarded it and came in ever greater numbers to settle on the Indian lands. The first settler arrived in 1769 and built his cabin close to the Watauga River.

A VARIETY OF GOVERNMENTS

In 1772 the people of the settlement organized the Watauga Association and elected a government, the first organized west of the Alleghenies. By 1775 the Indians had given up title to the land on which the settlement was growing. In 1776 the settlements in Tennessee requested to be annexed by the government of North Carolina. This led to the formation, in 1777, of Washington County of North Carolina, which included all of present Tennessee. A community named Jonesboro was laid out in 1779 as the county seat. This is the oldest town in Tennessee.

Many of the Indians were dissatisfied with the loss of their lands to the Watauga settlers. To take advantage of the American preoccupation with the Revolutionary War, the Indians went to war. Two years of fighting ensued. The Battle of Island Flats, 1776, occurred in what is now the business district of Kingston. After their defeat in this battle and others, the Indians met with representatives of North Carolina and Virginia in their sacred treaty place, Long Island, in the Holston River, and gave their word to keep peace.

One of the leaders, Dragging Canoe, still was dissatisfied. Along with other chiefs and many followers, Dragging Canoe broke away from the main Cherokee nation and set up villages to the west along Chickamauga Creek. The outlaw Indian group became known as the Chickamauga. Outlaw settlers joined them, and they made many raids on the remote settlements.

In 1779 Colonel Evan Shelby took a small army from Watauga to meet the Chickamauga. The army defeated the Indians near Chattanooga, burned villages, and scattered their people. The Chickamauga then moved farther to the south and set up new villages at Lookout Mountain.

In 1780 messengers brought news that British armies were moving westward to crush the American Revolution once and for all. The mountain men sprang to their arms and hurried across the ranges, led by John Sevier. On the seventh of October they took part in the Battle of Kings Mountain, South Carolina. They had learned the methods of Indian fighting well; their guerrilla tactics helped win the battle, one of the turning points of the Revolutionary War. It was the only formal battle of the Revolution in which forces from Tennessee took part.

Also in 1780, Fort Nashborough (Nashville) and other middle Tennessee settlements were begun, even though the war was still raging to the east. At this time Tennessee was almost as remote from the rest of civilization as if it had been on the moon. Tennessee settlers asked North Carolina to set up a suitable government, but the mother state did not feel able to govern such a far-off province. Tennessee was turned over to the central government, but it had no time for such matters.

Feeling deserted on every side, the people of Tennessee sent representatives to a convention at Jonesboro to set up a new government. It was to be known as the State of Franklin; in 1784 a constitu-

A part of old Fort Nashborough has been re-created in present-day Nashville.

tion was written, patterned after North Carolina's. John Sevier was elected governor of the infant state.

At about this same time, North Carolina changed its mind, set up a government for its western province, and sent officials in to represent it. There were constant clashes between supporters of the North Carolina representatives and proponents of the State of Franklin under Sevier. John Tipton, an opponent of Franklin, once met Sevier on the street of Jonesboro, and the two clashed in a fistfight before friends could separate them. For nonpayment of North Carolina taxes, officers of North Carolina seized some of Sevier's slaves. Sevier assembled a force of 150 men and marched over to the house where his slaves were being held. In the scuffle that followed, three men were killed, and when North Carolina reinforcements hurried up, Sevier was forced to retreat to Jonesboro.

After four years of wrangling, Governor John Sevier was seized by Tipton on charges of treason to North Carolina. Sevier's term expired; there were no new elections, and the State of Franklin ceased to exist. Greeneville had been its capital during its last two years. Tennessee was once more without a government, so the residents of the area formed what they called the Government South of the Holston and French Broad Rivers. It was patterned after the government of North Carolina and placed under the leadership of the former Franklin officials.

At last North Carolina gave up. On February 25,1790, it executed a deed of cession, which turned the Tennessee region over to the United States. This time, in 1790, the federal government established the Territory of the United States South of the River Ohio, generally called the Southwest Territory. William Blount was appointed the first territorial governor.

When Blount came to the territory, about the only suitable capitol building was the snug log-cabin home built by William Cobb near Johnson City. For the next eighteen months the cabin, called Rocky Mount, was the capitol of the first recognized government west of the Allegheny Mountains.

Knoxville was selected as territorial capital, and Governor Blount built the first frame house west of the Alleghenies as a combined executive mansion and capitol for the territory. The building, still standing, was finished in 1792.

LAST OF THE CHICKAMAUGA

For a time after the Revolutionary War, there were almost no Indian conflicts. A treaty made by Governor Blount opened up new regions for settlement and gave the settlers use of the Tennessee River and a road through Cherokee land. However, at a meeting in 1792, some members of the militia attacked the Indians, wounding Chief Hanging Maw and his wife and killing several others. The entire Cherokee nation joined with the Chickamauga and the Creek in a new war on the settlers.

A letter from Colonel Valentine Sevier to his brother, former Governor John Sevier, describes the terror and hardship of the times. "Dear Brother: The news from this place is desperate with me. On Tuesday, 11th of November [1794], last, about twelve o'clock my station [now New Providence] was attacked by about forty Indians. On so sudden a surprise they were in almost every house before they were discovered. All the men belonging to the station were out save only Snyder and myself. William Snyder, Betsy, his wife, his son John, and my son Joseph were killed in Snyder's house. They also killed Ann King and her son James, and scalped my daughter Rebecca. I hope she will still recover. The Indians have killed whole families about here this fall. You may hear the cries of some persons for their friends daily. The engagement commenced at my house continued about an hour, as the neighbors say. Such a scene no man ever witnessed before. Nothing but screams and the roaring of guns, and no man to assist me for some time."

Nashville and other communities also suffered Indian attacks. At last, Major James Ore gathered a large force and marched into Chickamauga territory. A bloody battle took place at the Indian town of Nickajack, near South Pittsburg. Taken by surprise, the Indians were beaten. Their towns Nickajack and Running Water were destroyed. By the end of 1794, the power of the Cherokee was

William Blount, the first territorial governor, built this first frame house west of the Alleghenies as a combined executive mansion and capitol for the Southwest Territory.

broken; the Chickamauga were dissolved as a separate group and returned to the main Cherokee body.

STATEHOOD

Despite the Indian conflicts, the territory grew. In 1782 General James Robertson set up a depot at Memphis to aid the Chickasaw Indians against the Spanish, who were anxious to extend their settlements into American territory east of the Mississippi.

The Spanish had built forts at Memphis as early as 1739. In 1795 Spanish Fort San Fernando de Las Barrancas was built near the corner of what is now Auction Avenue and Front Street in Memphis. But, fearing American attack, the Spanish soon moved the fort to their territory across the Mississippi. Later, Americans, including Captain Zebulon M. Pike, built other forts in the vicinity.

By 1796 the population of Tennessee was above the number necessary for a new state. A convention met at Knoxville to draw up a constitution, described by Thomas Jefferson as the "least imperfect and most republican" of any state constitution. Knoxville was chosen as temporary first capital.

When Congress did not act promptly to admit Tennessee as a state, Tennesseans elected John Sevier as governor, and the legislature chose William Blount and William Cocke as United States senators. Youthful, temperamental Andrew Jackson was elected as the first congressman.

Congress finally acted, and on June 1, 1796, Tennessee became the sixteenth state, the second to be created from the Southwest Territory. At first Blount and Cocke were refused their seats because they had been elected before Tennessee was a state. But Tennesseans soon reelected them.

Only a year later, Blount was connected with a serious scandal. He was accused of treason in trying to help the British cause against France in a war between the two nations. Although Blount was impeached, he was never tried because of his tremendous popularity in the frontier regions.

This capitol mural shows the advance of settlement in Tennessee.

Yesterday and Today

STIRRING TIMES

After statehood, settlers continued to pour in, struggling over the mountain gaps, floating on flatboats down the Ohio and up the Tennessee and Cumberland rivers. By the turn of the century, Tennessee had almost ceased to be a frontier.

Another scandal rocked the state when John Sevier was accused of fraud in connection with land grants. He had served three successive terms as governor and was prohibited by the state constitution from serving a fourth. Archibald Roane had become the second governor. In spite of the scandal, the extremely popular Sevier ran for governor in 1803 and was elected.

One of the mysteries of American history occurred near Hohenwald. On October 11, 1809, western explorer Meriwether Lewis met his death at an inn known as Grinder's Stand. He had been traveling along the old Natchez Trace road from the Louisiana Territory, where he was governor, to Washington. The death is officially a suicide, but many authorities feel that Lewis was murdered. A number of important papers that he had with him have never been found.

Andrew Jackson gained national fame as a leader in the Indian wars of the southeast, in which he subdued the Creek. Camp Blount near Fayetteville was a mustering site for troops in this war.

Soon after, toward the close of the War of 1812, Tennessee troops again assembled at Camp Blount, this time to take part in the Battle of New Orleans, where their help was extremely important. Again they fought under Andrew Jackson. One of the most notable forced marches of military history was undertaken by Tennessee volunteers under General John Coffee. They are said to have marched 120 miles (312 kilometers) in two days and two nights in order to reach New Orleans in time for the battle.

When word of Andrew Jackson's victory at New Orleans reached his home town of Jonesboro, it was said that he not only had killed all the British soldiers in the battle but had immediately set sail to conquer England as well.

One enthusiast heard the victory news and shouted, "Whoopee! Hurrah for Andy Jackson! Hell-and-thunder, I knowed he could whip anybody the day I seed him ride that hoss-race at Greasy Cove!" The phrase "Andy Jackson, hell-and-thunder" is still used to express excitement in the Jonesboro region.

Murfreesboro became the capital in 1819 and continued in that position until 1825. Also in 1819 the first steamboat puffed up the Cumberland River to Nashville. Nine years later Knoxville went wild over its first steamboat. Another occasion for celebration was the visit of the Marquis de Lafayette, French hero of the American Revolution. Nashville gave the hero a great banquet, and he visited Andrew Jackson at the Hermitage.

A SAD CHAPTER

During the early years of the century, most of the Indians of Tennessee adopted the ways of the settlers. They studied the most scientific farming methods of the day, improved the roads in their territory, grew and wove cotton, and even owned slaves. Their homes were as fine as their neighbors'.

The Cherokee wrote their own constitution in 1827 for an independent nation on the 10 million acres (4 million hectares) they still owned in three states.

Because of the greed and envy of others this was not to be. Settlers were constantly trying to gain "legal" control of the Indian lands. As early as 1818 the Chickasaw had given up all their West Tennessee lands except for four square miles (ten square kilometers), and even this was signed away in 1823.

The United States Supreme Court upheld the Cherokee rights, but Andrew Jackson, then president, refused to honor the solemn treaties sworn by the United States. Congress and the president tried to persuade the Cherokee to exchange their lands for western territory, but they refused.

In 1835, however, a minority of the Cherokee signed a treaty giving up their lands for $5 million and 15 million acres (6 million hec-

Cherokee leader John Ross. Painting by Charles Byrd King.

tares) in the West. Cherokee leader John Ross said this was not the wish of the majority, but the government was determined to act without majority consent. Troops were sent to round up the Indians, and in 1838 they were marched out of their ancestral lands on the road to the West. The route became known as the Trail of Tears, because of the suffering endured by the Indians.

THE VOLUNTEER STATE

Nashville became the permanent capital of Tennessee in 1843.

Three years later the war with Mexico gave Tennessee its nickname. The government called for twenty-eight hundred volunteers from Tennessee. The response was overwhelming, with more than thirty thousand answering the call. Tennessee became known as the Volunteer State.

31

PRELUDE TO DISASTER

The people of Tennessee were active in the growing dispute over slavery. In 1796, the year the Constitution was ratified, two thousand people had signed a petition calling for the emancipation of all slaves by 1864. Compared with others, Tennessee's slave code was liberal, guaranteeing clothing and food as well as shelter and medical care. It provided for the care of elderly slaves, gave slaves the right to trial by jury, and allowed them to make contracts for their freedom.

East Tennessee, with small landholders and few slaves, was opposed to slavery. One of the first abolition magazines was started in 1819 by Thomas Embree at Jonesboro. By 1827 East Tennessee had about a fifth of the total number of antislavery societies in the United States.

However, there were many slaves in Middle Tennessee and even larger numbers in the western section. These regions were strongly in favor of slavery, and so it may be said that by 1855 Tennessee was a slave state.

Despite this fact, the people of Tennessee at first voted against secession, when other Southern states seceded from the Union. After President Abraham Lincoln called for troops to subdue the seceding states, however, Governor Isham G. Harris wrote, "Tennessee will not furnish a single man for coercion, but 50,000, if necessary, for the defense of our rights or those of our Southern brethren." When another vote was taken a few months later, the majority elected to secede. Tennessee was the last state to do so.

Led by Andrew Johnson, Horace Maynard, and others, a convention of East Tennessee Unionists met to protest the secession of their state.

Irked by the Union sentiment in East Tennessee, Governor Isham G. Harris wrote: "We can temporize with the rebellious spirit of that people no longer.... The arrest and indictment for treason of the ringleaders will give perfect peace and quiet to that division of our State in the course of two months." A Confederate force of more than ten thousand was sent to East Tennessee, with headquarters in

Knoxville, and took over the region. More than fifteen hundred Union sympathizers were sent to jail, and hundreds more fled to safety in Union-held Kentucky.

President Lincoln lamented: "My distress is that our friends in East Tennessee are being hanged and driven to despair, and even now, I fear, are thinking of taking rebel arms for the sake of personal protection. In this we lose the most valuable stake we have in the South." However, at that time little could be done about the situation.

A STATE OF WAR

Confederate President Jefferson Davis chose Leonidas Polk as commander in Tennessee, with Albert Sidney Johnston in charge of the western department. Late in January, 1862, General Ulysses S. Grant perfected a plan to break the eleven-mile (eighteen-kilometer) Confederate line between Forts Henry (on the Tennessee River) and Donelson (on the Cumberland), opening up an avenue into the heart of the Confederacy by way of the river valleys.

The forces of Fort Henry withdrew before they were surrounded, but Fort Donelson withstood Grant's attack for a time. Then on February 16, 1862, Confederate General Simon B. Buckner agreed to Grant's demand for unconditional and immediate surrender of Fort Donelson. Grant captured 13,500 men, 3,000 horses, and 20,000 muskets. Grant's victory gave courage to the North and caused great damage to the South.

Federal forces also advanced on Nashville; the state government fled to Memphis; and on February 23, 1862, the capital city surrendered to Federal forces. President Lincoln appointed Andrew Johnson military governor of Tennessee.

General Grant began to move south, stopping at Pittsburg Landing to wait for reinforcements. At the same time General Johnston made an eighteen-mile (twenty-nine kilometer) march with forty thousand Confederate troops to surprise Grant. On April 6, 1862, Johnston attacked Grant's forces at the site of Shiloh Church, south-

A Henry Lewis illustration of early Memphis. During the Civil War, Memphis residents watched history's first battle between the boats known as "rams."

west of Pittsburg Landing. The Federal forces were forced to withdraw. As the day went on, General Johnston was hit in the artery of a leg by a rifle shot and bled to death. Because of this loss and Grant's murderous artillery fire, the Confederate attack halted.

That night Generals Buell and Wallace brought reinforcements to Grant, who attacked in the morning and forced the Confederates to retreat. Neither side could claim a victory. The death toll mounted to twenty-five thousand men; losses on both sides were about equal. The Battle of Shiloh was the second major battle of the entire war.

On June 6, 1862, a Federal fleet bore down on Memphis and sank or captured every Confederate boat except one. Most of the people of the city watched the battle in fascination from the bluff. It was history's first battle between the boats known as "rams." Commodore C.H. Davis took over the city and raised the Stars and Stripes over the post office.

The Battle of Stones River (Murfreesboro), from December 31, 1862, through January 2, 1863, was one of the hardest fought battles of the war. Union forces were commanded by General William S. Rosecrans, assisted by Generals Philip A. Sheridan and George H. Thomas. Federal forces lost thirteen thousand; and Confederate dead numbered ten thousand. But the way was opened for the Union advance southward to Chattanooga, which fell in September of 1863.

Later in September, at Chickamauga Creek in Georgia, a few miles south of Chattanooga, Federal forces suffered a disaster. But the Confederate troops were not able to follow up the victory because of the defense of Union General George H. Thomas, the Rock of Chickamauga. The Federal army retreated northward into Chattanooga, and the victorious Confederate army laid siege to the city.

By November, the Federal forces, under Grant, had sufficient reinforcements to resume the offensive. They moved toward Lookout Mountain, making an almost impossible climb up the steep sides. They met Confederate forces on November 24. Because of the fog and mist that swirled about, this fight has become known as the Battle above the Clouds. To keep from being cut off from their main force on Missionary Ridge, the Confederate forces left the Lookout Mountain battle. The next day Northern armies attacked Missionary Ridge and forced a Southern retreat into Georgia.

Chattanooga became the base from which General Sherman made his march through Georgia.

Also in late 1863 Union forces at Knoxville suffered a destructive siege. But the city held out, and Confederate forces finally withdrew.

The year 1864 found most of Tennessee in Federal control but under constant threat of raids by Confederate forces. Many of the attacks were led by Confederate General Nathan Bedford Forrest. He became known as the Gadfly, because he dashed in and flew

35

away before he could be captured. One of his most spectacular raids struck Memphis in August.

One of Forrest's raids was unique. On November 4, 1864, he attacked the Federal supply base at Johnsonville on the Tennessee River. By the next morning almost nothing remained of the base. Included in the destruction were thirty gunboats, transports, and barges. This is the only known defeat of a naval force by cavalry.

In the Battle of Lookout Mountain (known as the Battle above the Clouds) Union forces drove Confederate forces from the mountain and soon captured Chattanooga. From there, General Sherman began his march through Georgia.

THE STAGGERING TOLL

In late 1864, Confederate General Thomas Hood was ordered to strike at central Tennessee, capture Nashville, and separate the Federal troops from their supplies. Not far from Nashville, Federal troops under General John Schofield, trying to reinforce General George H. Thomas in the city, were attacked by Hood near Franklin. The Battle of Franklin is said to rank with the Battle of Stalingrad in World War II as one of the bloodiest in modern history. In the short period of only fifty-five minutes, 8,528 men lost their lives. This loss included more officers than had been killed in any other single battle. The Confederate forces alone lost six generals. Confederate dead numbered 6,202 and Union 2,326. Schofield hurried on to Nashville.

On December 15, General Thomas attacked and almost destroyed Hood's army.

A huge number of battles and skirmishes occurred in Tennessee during the war. Some estimates place the number at three hundred; others go as high as seven hundred.

Before the end of the war, a total of 217,744 Tennesseans had become members of the armed services. Of these, 186,652 were on the Confederate side, and 31,092 were on the Union side.

Cities were in ashes, countless homes destroyed, families uprooted. One observer remarked, "The progress of seventy-five years had been wiped out by four years of war."

AFTERMATH

After the war Tennessee entered what some have called a second pioneer period.

One of Tennessee's distinctions came on February 25, 1865, when the people approved a state constitutional amendment freeing the slaves. Tennessee was the only state to do this by popular vote.

Three days later, Andrew Johnson resigned his position as military governor and became vice president of the United States under Abraham Lincoln.

Unscrupulous people both from the North and from the local population tried to take advantage of unsettled conditions. One of the worst was A.E. Alden, a Northerner who managed to be elected mayor of Nashville. The "Alden Ring" bled the city by issuing notes and bills on the city's credit and by every other means they could find.

Many from both North and South truly tried to help the freed slaves. Others took every advantage of them, and some tried to stir them to riot and other violence. The Ku Klux Klan was formed at Pulaski under the leadership of former Confederate soldiers. With weird costumes, secret meetings, threats, beatings, and lynchings, the Klan sought to intimidate and control the blacks.

As early as 1865 President Andrew Johnson proclaimed the end of Tennessee's insurrection. But Congress did not readmit the state to the Union until March 23, 1866.

Conditions began to improve with the administration of Governor DeWitt C. Senter in 1869. He helped end the military occupation of the state and pardoned many military prisoners of war.

A convention was called in 1870, with John C. Brown as its president. Brown set a high tone in his opening remarks: "Let us raise ourselves above the passions and prejudices of the hour, and dare to be just and generous regardless of the temptations prompting a contrary course. We cannot, we must not, be unmindful of the great changes that have impressed themselves upon our history. Let us accept the situation, and not seek to alter circumstances which have passed beyond our control." The new constitution restored the vote to Tennessee men who had lost it during the Reconstruction. It also included Negro suffrage.

In 1871 Brown became the first Democratic governor since the war.

PROBLEMS AND PROGRESS

After the war the people of Tennessee suffered greatly from disease. Nashville was almost deserted during the cholera epidemic of

1866. Throngs left the city in 1873 when cholera struck once more. One newspaper advised, "Use sulphur in your socks, one-half teaspoonful in each sock every morning. This will charge your system with sulphurated hydrogen which is a bar to cholera." In spite of this "cure" more than a thousand died. June 20, the date when seventy-two died, has been known as Black Friday ever since.

Memphis had yellow fever epidemics in 1866 and 1873. The worst was in 1878—the city was almost depopulated. As the disease progressed, 25,000 persons left the city in two weeks. Scenes of horror followed. Deaths mounted and the streets were deserted except for the hearse. Of course, at that time the cause of yellow fever was not known, and proper sanitation was also unknown. Relief did not come until frost killed the mosquitoes that spread the disease. More than five thousand people lost their lives.

One of the most unusual political campaigns took place in 1886. Two brothers, Alfred A. Taylor, Republican, and Robert Love Taylor, Democrat, sought the governorship. Alf's supporters wore red roses, Bob's wore white roses, and the campaign came to be called the War of the Roses. They campaigned together and spoke from the same platform.

On one occasion Bob stole Alf's speech and delivered it before his brother had the chance. Robert Taylor won the election, and Alfred had to wait until 1920 for his chance to become governor.

The state had its first major strike in 1891, in the Coal Creek region. When the mine companies tried to use convict labor to work the mines, miners forced the convicts out on several occasions. After numerous clashes between miners and militia, the public became aroused. The law that permitted convicts to be leased for work was overthrown.

A Centennial Exposition was staged at Nashville in 1897. President William McKinley in Washington pressed a button that fired a cannon to open the fair. Later the president visited the exposition.

A sad and strange event of 1908 was the assassination of former Senator Edward Ward Carmack, who was opposing Malcolm R. Patterson for the governorship. Friends of Patterson, Duncan Cooper and his son Robin, shot Carmack and left him dead on the streets of

Nashville. Duncan Cooper was found guilty and sentenced to death for the crime, but when Patterson became governor, he gave his friend a full pardon.

World War I brought fame to a native of Tennessee, Sergeant Alvin C. York. York killed more than 20 German soldiers and forced 132 more to surrender. Probably the best-known enlisted man of the war, he was awarded the Congressional Medal of Honor.

Tennessee lived up to its reputation as the Volunteer State when 91,180 Tennesseans enlisted in the armed forces. Thirty-four hundred lost their lives. Approximately 400,000 were engaged in war work at home.

A MODERN STATE

In 1920 the state legislature approved the Nineteenth Amendment to the Constitution. It was the final ratification needed to put the amendment into operation, and it gave American women the vote.

Under Governor Austin Peay's administration, 1923-1927, the state government was almost completely reorganized. Almost fifty departments and bureaus were consolidated into eight major departments. During this time the principal highway developments of the state were begun, as well as plans for Great Smoky Mountains National Park.

World attention focused on Tennessee in 1925. In that year a law had been passed forbidding the teaching of the theory of evolution in any school supported by state funds. Dayton science teacher John T. Scopes decided to test the law and admitted that he had taught the theory of evolution in his classes. His trial, the "Monkey Trial," received tremendous publicity.

Attorney Clarence Darrow led the defense of Scopes, and political leader William Jennings Bryan headed the prosecution. After one of the best-publicized trials in history, Scopes was declared guilty and fined a hundred dollars. Bryan, the victorious attorney, died only five days after the close of the trial. The Scopes trial has been the subject of books, plays, and motion pictures.

Attorney Clarence Darrow (left) defended science teacher John T. Scopes in the 1925 "Monkey Trial." William Jennings Bryan (right) was the prosecutor.

One of the greatest federal projects of the thirties was the Tennessee Valley Authority, set up to protect and to develop the natural resources of the Tennessee Valley by providing hydroelectric power to the region. TVA has been called "one of the wonders of the Twentieth Century," as well as "one of the greatest threats to free enterprise and the American way of life."

Most will agree, however, that TVA has developed the Tennessee River system for navigation, flood control, and power generation, making the Tennessee one of the most useful rivers in the world. The program has given Tennessee Valley farmers a tool for building new farming systems to conserve soil and water and help increase farm income.

Working with state forestry agencies and timberland owners, TVA has helped advance reforestation, fire control, and management practices to restore woodlands. TVA dams have created a channel 650 miles (1,040 kilometers) long and deep enough to give inland barges and towboats year-round access to a waterway system connecting more than twenty states. Locks at these dams handle 13 million tons (nearly 12 million metric tons) of freight traffic annually.

Low-cost power from TVA has created opportunities for important manufacturing processes that require large amounts of electricity. There is a bonus benefit from the lakes. They have made Tennessee one of the most popular recreation areas in the country.

The first major project of TVA was Norris Dam, begun in 1933. Three years later the dam began to back up the waters to form the mighty Norris Lake.

A not-so-happy river event was the great flood of 1937, the worst ever to terrorize the Mississippi River area. Memphis had the stupendous job of caring for almost sixty thousand refugees. Memphis's "Boss" Edward Hall Crump was one of the most deter-

Norris Dam, begun in 1933, was the first major project of the Tennessee Valley Authority.

mined workers during the crises. When a member of a chain gang working on the levees asked another if he thought the levee would break, the answer was "No." The reason was, "Mister Crump says it won't."

World War II found 315,501 Tennesseans in service; 7,727 lost their lives.

During the war, Tennessee was the center of what has been called the best-kept secret in history. When the frantic race for the secret of the atomic bomb proved successful, the government selected Oak Ridge as the site for its atomic energy plant. The first uranium chain-reactor was placed in operation at Clinton Laboratories, known now as the Oak Ridge National Laboratory. Thousands of workers were brought in; elaborate installations were erected almost overnight, and only a handful of people had the slightest idea why so many hundreds of millions of dollars were being spent with such haste. Fewer still could have imagined the end product—a weapon that would completely destroy two Japanese cities, bring an end to the war, and usher in the atomic age.

Most of the advances since the war have been concerned with growth of industry, agriculture, transportation, and communication, all covered in later sections.

The decade of the sixties marked noteworthy advances in the struggle for civil rights but there was tragedy, as well. Martin Luther King, Jr., an outstanding leader in the civil rights movement, was assassinated in Memphis in April, 1968. James Earl Ray was sentenced to 99 years' imprisonment for the crime.

The fifties and sixties also saw the rise of country and western music, headquartered at Nashville. Elvis Presley, the king of rock and roll, made his home in Memphis until his death in 1977.

THE PEOPLE OF TENNESSEE

"The secret of America's strength," wrote Supreme Court Justice William O. Douglas, "was in people like those in Cades Cove." In the little community of Cades Cove, nestled in the Great Smoky

Mountains National Park, are preserved some of the customs of Tennessee mountain life, now rapidly vanishing. It is less and less true, as a mountain man remarked, that a person "has got to scratch and sweat mightily if he wants to starve decent."

In earlier times people had to make do with what they could create by their own ingenuity. Gourds served, and still serve in some places, a multitude of uses. The larger ones stored lard, homemade soap, or other materials; long-handled gourds became dippers and ladles.

Pioneers built their houses themselves, but all the neighbors for miles around would pitch in to help. In some houses every board was carefully mitered, spliced, and pegged. Kegs were hollowed from three-foot sections of tree trunks, and feed troughs also were hollowed from oak trunks. Even hinges were whittled out of wood. Once the house was built and fireplace finished, the hearth fire, in which all the cooking was done, would be kept lit continually. One hearth fire that had burned for three generations finally was extinguished by waters from a TVA dam.

Many mountain people became very skilled in craft work. With the coming of manufactured goods, handicrafts were in danger of dying out. But several individuals and groups made tremendous efforts to teach and encourage the people in handicrafts. Today Tennessee craft workers turn out chairs, ceramics, jewelry, weaving, baskets, dolls, games, toys, carvings, and other woodcraft.

A majority of the early settlers were English, Scottish, and Scotch-Irish. Most other nationalities followed, but in smaller numbers. Some stayed in communities of their own such as the Swiss colony of Gruetli. Today, about seventy thousand residents of Tennessee are foreign born, according to the 1970 census. The largest group is from Germany, and the next largest from Canada and the United Kingdom.

The black population of Tennessee is 621,000 or about 15.8 percent of the total population.

Within the past twenty-five years, the status of blacks in Tennessee has changed for the better and blacks now occupy prestigious positions in both government and the private sector.

Tennessee craft workers are skilled in wood carving (left) and pottery making (above), as well as many other crafts.

Among the country's most unusual ethnic groups are the Irish Nomads, descendants of four families of horse traders who came to America in 1875. The Nomads were noted for their annual gathering in Nashville, at which burial services were held for all those who had died in the preceding year. The graves are at Mt. Calvary Cemetery, Lebanon Road.

Organized religion quickly followed the settlers into the new country. The first Methodist conference to be formed west of the Alleghenies was organized at Half Acres by Bishop Francis Asbury in 1778.

One of the most spectacular religious movements was the Great Revival, which began around 1800 and swept the entire region. Revival meetings sometimes continued for weeks, with stirring preaching and huge crowds.

A small but influential denomination, the Cumberland Presbyterian Church, was born in Tennessee near White Bluff in 1810. It is headquartered in Memphis.

45

Right: The iris is the state flower.
Below: Roan Mountain is blanketed with a huge natural garden of blooming rhododendron.

Natural Treasures

GROWING THINGS

One of the most magnificent scenes of nature is in East Tennessee. The almost treeless, gently sloping summit of Roan Mountain is blanketed with a 600-acre (240-hectare) natural garden of purple rhododendron. At the peak of bloom, the entire mountain bursts into color.

One of the showiest flowering shrubs is the flame azalea. When the mists sweep across the highlands and the tourist cannot see the road because of fog, a cluster of flame azalea may show up on the hillside like a beacon. The mountain laurel is another lovely bloom of the higher country.

In the Smokies 3,710 varieties of plant life grow. There is a larger number of flowers and ferns thriving in Tennessee than anywhere else in the world in an equal area.

One of the most spectacular is the wild tiger lily, with flower stalks sometimes reaching 6 feet (1.8 meters) in height.

The delicate iris is the state flower.

More than 150 varieties of trees grow in Tennessee. One of the country's most tremendous stands of virgin hardwoods covers 200,000 acres (80,000 hectares) in the Smokies. Included are 50,000 acres (20,000 hectares) of red spruce, some more than four hundred years old. The largest tree in the Smokies is the yellow poplar, or tulip tree, which may grow to be 9 feet (3 meters) across and 200 feet (60 meters) high.

Government protection is given to the timber resources in Cherokee National Forest and in Cedars of Lebanon State Park, the largest remaining stand of red cedar in the United States.

Among Tennessee's unusual trees are the rare Chinquapin and the yellow wood, or gopher tree.

Many a deep woodland or roadside is brightened in spring by redbud and dogwood blossoms.

Tennessee's carpet of bluegrass, covering 4 million acres (1.6 million hectares), is some of the world's most prized pasture.

CREATURES OF SKY, WATER, LAND

One of the most popular wild beasts anywhere is the Smoky Mountain bear. Wherever long lines of cars are seen parked on the mountain roads, visitors can be almost certain that a bear is raiding a roadside trash can. When these animals become too surly or troublesome, they have to be rounded up in a trailer cage and taken off to a faraway section.

The bear is also a popular game animal, as are the deer and the Russian wild boars. These were imported by a hunting club and have become great favorites with game hunters.

Popular game birds are the haughty grouse, many kinds of ducks, geese, quail, and the magnificent wild turkey. Old-time turkey shoots, with flintlock rifles, are popular in the mountains.

Bird life in Tennessee may be more varied than in any other state. There are 316 species. Among the many haunts of the great blue heron, the heronry at Reelfoot Lake is one of the largest anywhere. Almost every type of swimming or wading fowl can be found around Reelfoot.

The state bird, the mockingbird, still is plentiful, but many other birds that once numbered in the millions are extinct. The passenger pigeon, ivorybilled woodpecker, prairie chicken, Cumberland parrot, and others are gone. The spectacular bald eagle is seen in only a few remote spots, as is the northern raven.

The Smoky Mountain bear is one of the most popular wild animals anywhere.

Bird life in Tennessee is varied. These bluejays enjoy a meal.

Tennessee is known as a fisherman's paradise. Popular varieties include brown, rainbow, and brook trout, bass of many types, bluegill, walleye, sauger, muskellunge, catfish, and red horse. Among the unusual species are the strange alligator gar, unchanged from prehistoric times, and the spoonbill catfish.

Reelfoot Lake is known as America's greatest natural fish hatchery, where more than fifty-six varieties of fish are found. In Snail Shell Cave, near Murfreesboro, seventeen different kinds of snails have been identified.

MINERAL TREASURES

One of the country's great coal reserves is in Tennessee's Cumberland Plateau region, covering 4,400 square miles (11,440 square kilometers). More copper is found in the copper basin of East Tennessee than in any other state east of the Mississippi. Phosphate, clay, and zinc are also found in worthwhile amounts.

Few states have more distinctive building stone. Tennessee Marble, renowned for its quality, is found in twenty varieties. Except for white, every color of marble is found in Tennessee, including one of almost jet black tone. Sewanee sandstone has beautiful pink shading. Crab Orchard sandstone—with patterns of brown—is quite rare.

People Use Their Treasures

MANUFACTURING AND MINING

Tennessee ranks second in manufacturing in the southeastern United States, producing about $8 billion annually. Chemicals, food and related products, apparel, electrical machinery, textiles, stone, clay, and glass are the leading products.

This vast outpouring of manufactured goods is a big change from the time when the milling of grain brought in by settlers was the only industry except farming. If an early Tennessean wanted something, he usually had to make it himself.

In the old days, lye soap was made at home. Wood ashes were carefully saved, as were scraps of fat meat. The meat scraps and lye, made from the wood ashes, were then boiled together in large iron kettles. The most experienced soap maker, generally a grandmother, decided how long to boil the mixture. Then the soap was poured and cooled. Homemade soap did more than remove dirt. It was strong enough to take off a good deal of skin too, unless much care was used.

Tennessee was an iron-making state in the early days; there were twenty-nine iron furnaces in the Bristol region alone at one time. Because of limited ore supplies, the importance of this industry has dwindled in recent times.

However, Tennessee is a leader in one of the most important metal industries of the space age—aluminum. Alcoa, the industrial city of Aluminum Company of America, is the center of a giant aluminum manufacturing enterprise. Aluminum making requires enormous amounts of electricity; the aluminum industry is greatly strengthened by the inexpensive hydroelectric power of the region.

One of the smaller but more interesting industries is handicrafts, encouraged by various guilds. The fine handmade products of the state are much sought after by tourists.

Among Tennessee's most interesting manufacturing establishments is the skewer factory at Jackson, the world's largest producer of lollipop sticks, flower props, clothespins, and other stick products.

The principal mineral industry of the state is the mining and processing of marble, limestone, and zinc. Tennessee is among the leading states in the production of phosphate.

Annual mining production amounts to about $300 million.

AGRICULTURE AND LUMBER

Although farm income is now far below that of manufacturing, Tennessee's farms are still important. Total income from agriculture exceeds $1.5 billion. Of this, $700 million comes from crops and the rest from livestock.

Tennessee ranks sixth in the United States in tobacco production. Burley tobacco is grown in great quantities in East Tennessee, and Middle and West Tennessee also produce tobacco of high quality. Greeneville, Clarksville, and Springfield are leading tobacco centers. Their warehouses echo with the singsong chant of the tobacco auctioneer.

In 1966 the state ranked sixth in cotton production, accounting for 670,000 bales. But production has declined. As a cash crop, cotton is no longer the leading income producer of Tennessee agriculture.

A forage crop of growing importance in the United States—lespedeza—was introduced to this country in Tennessee.

One of the most interesting products of Tennessee farms is thoroughbred horses. The vast acreage of bluegrass country provides an ideal environment for raising the finest horses. Tennessee gave the world the Tennessee Walking Horse, which has been called the world's greatest pleasure horse. This wonderful animal originated in the central basin of Middle Tennessee. Horse farms in this area are also noted for Tennessee American saddle horses and the American standardbred horse. Aberdeen Angus and shorthorns are popular breeds of beef cattle in Tennessee. The largest breed, however, is Hereford, and one of the three finest Hereford farms in the country is located in the state.

The vast and beautiful forests of Tennessee produce materials amounting to almost $1 billion annually. Hardwood flooring is among the most important wood products; Tennessee is the leading producer of such flooring.

TRANSPORTATION AND COMMUNICATION

At first, overland travel in Tennessee followed the network of Indian trails. The most famous of these was the great Natchez Trace, leading from Nashville to Natchez, Mississippi. During the late 1700s the Natchez Trace became an important highway. French traders and missionaries traveled it; later the English used it, and then the Spanish. After 1800, Indians, explorers, and hunters were followed by circuit-riding preachers, soldiers, government agents, and settlers.

Another famous trail was the Great Indian Warpath, which came into Tennessee near Chattanooga, then went north up the valley of the Tennessee. In 1775 Daniel Boone pioneered the Wilderness Road; stagecoach service between Nashville and Memphis began in 1829, and the state had its first macadam road two years later.

Also important in the history of travel were the suspension bridge over the Cumberland River, built in 1850 at Nashville, and the three-mile (five-kilometer) bridge over the Mississippi at Memphis, constructed in 1892. In recent years about a thousand miles (1600 kilometers) of interstate superhighways have been added to the state's regular network of roads.

Tennessee was the first state to adopt a law ordering the inspection and grading of every hotel and eating place.

Rivers always have been important routes of travel and trade. Even in the days of flatboats, the rivers carried a large volume of freight.

The steamboat boom made the rivers even more important. All up and down the major rivers of the state went stately river packets, showboats, and floating department stores.

Although the steamboat days are over, modern towboats and barges carry a larger load of freight than did the old steamboats. The dams of the Tennessee Valley Authority provide the world's most

52

The Delta Queen *of Memphis brings back memories of the early days when showboats traveled up and down the state's major rivers.*

fully regulated river system. At TVA dams, huge locks lift barge tows from one lake to the next on their "stair-step" trip up the Tennessee River waterway.

Using a computer to calculate stream flows from rainfall readings across a seven-state region, TVA engineers control the flow of the river in much the same way a dispatcher controls train movements. All along the Tennessee and its tributaries, floodwaters are caught and stored by dams. All the major dams have hydroelectric installations that harness the power of falling water for the region's homes, farms, and industries.

Because of the fine waterways, Tennessee was not as anxious as other states to build railroads. In 1836 the state legislature offered to subsidize railroads, and the La Grange and Memphis built a ten-mile (sixteen-kilometer) experimental line out of Memphis. The first train ran in 1842, but the road failed. Not until 1851 was the Nashville and Chattanooga Railroad operating regularly. The first publication devoted entirely to promoting railroads in the United States was published at Rogersville in 1831. This was the *Railroad Advocate.*

The *Knoxville Gazette,* published at Rogersville on November 5, 1791, was Tennessee's first newspaper. Mark Twain's *Journalism in Tennessee* told of whippings, fistfights, duels, and other brawls among the newspaper editors of the state, who were noted for being rugged individuals—brawling and outspoken.

Today, one of the largest manufacturers of books in the world is the Kingsport Press, at Kingsport.

Human Treasures

HEWED FROM A HICKORY TRUNK

The foremost citizen in Tennessee history was not a native of Tennessee. He was Andrew Jackson, known as Old Hickory. According to one source, "For more than three decades the history of Tennessee was the history of Andrew Jackson"—a strange, hot-tempered man of vast ambition.

At the age of twenty-one, Jackson was sent to newly created Nashville to be attorney for what was then the western district of North Carolina. Beginning his political life as the state's first congressman, he then moved on to the United States Senate. Next he became a judge of the Tennessee Supreme Court.

In 1805 he got into a quarrel with Charles Dickinson over a horse race. The quarrel grew heated, and finally Jackson challenged Dickinson to a duel. It had to take place in Kentucky because Tennessee had a law against dueling. Jackson's gun at first failed to fire, and he was shot. But finally Jackson managed to fire his gun, and Dickinson was killed.

This was only one of Jackson's many duels. He had many quarrels with Governor John Sevier. In 1803 he challenged Sevier to a duel, which Sevier refused because of the antidueling law. Finally they met in a kind of mock duel. Neither man was hurt, and both left the field swearing at one another.

Because of Dickinson's death and the quarrel with Sevier, Jackson's career seemed at an end. But with his great successes in the Indian wars and his unparalleled victory at New Orleans, he became one of the best-known and best-liked men of the country.

In the presidential election of 1824, he received more electoral votes than any other candidate, but he did not get a majority. The House of Representatives chose John Quincy Adams over Jackson. Four years later, Jackson easily won the presidency.

Just before his inauguration, Jackson's beloved wife, Rachel, died. She had had a difficult life. She had separated from her first husband, and when she and Jackson were married, they thought her divorce had been finalized. It was not until almost two years later that Rachel's divorce actually was granted. When the Jacksons learned of this, they were remarried legally. Jackson's political opponents made the most of this "scandal" at every opportunity, and Jackson constantly was forced to defend his wife's reputation. Rachel suffered greatly from this situation, and also from her husband's constant scrapes.

Jackson's two terms in the White House were stormy ones, after which he retired to his home, the Hermitage, near Nashville. Jackson's personal choice for the presidency was his successor, Martin Van Buren. Until his death in 1845 Jackson continued to be a great force in national politics. James K. Polk, who became president in 1845, was one of Jackson's followers and was also Jackson's choice for the presidency.

Jackson was such a colorful personality that a host of anecdotes are told about him. One of these concerns the Hermitage Church, which Jackson built opposite the Hermitage to please his wife. At one time the church needed a new roof. The minister visited Jackson just as a gamecock fight was about to begin. Knowing that Jackson enjoyed a bet, the minister quickly said, "I'll wager you a new church roof that this bird wins," pointing to his choice. Jackson agreed with a smile; he knew the cocks were quite evenly matched.

The minister's fowl appeared to be losing, and Jackson yelled, "Remember, the church needs a roof." The bird seemed to revive and finally won. Jackson provided the new roof.

TWO PRESIDENTS

Andrew Johnson was greatly influenced by Tennessee, and the state in turn was much influenced by him. Johnson's family brought him to Greeneville when he was seventeen. Before many months had passed, the youthful tailor had made up all the cloth in town into suits and moved on to Rutledge. On his return to Greeneville, he married Eliza McCardle. It was she who taught the ambitious young man to read and do arithmetic.

Andrew Johnson came with his parents to Greeneville when he was an ambitious seventeen-year-old tailor. Entering politics, Johnson became an alderman, a mayor, a congressman, governor, vice president, and, finally, president of the United States.

Turning to politics, Johnson became first an alderman, next mayor, then a congressman, and finally governor of Tennessee from 1853 to 1857. When retiring Governor Campbell went to Johnson's hotel to take the new governor to his inauguration, Johnson said he preferred to walk with the people. Remembering his own struggle for an education, Johnson's first act as governor was to request aid for Tennessee education.

When war came, Johnson was in the United States Senate and remained loyal to the Union—the only Southern senator to do so. His loyalty was rewarded when he was appointed military governor of the state and then when he became vice president under Abraham Lincoln. When Johnson took the presidency after Lincoln's assassination, there was much consternation among Northerners who distrusted a Southerner in the White House, and equal dismay among Southerners who hated a Southern Unionist.

57

Pictures on this page were taken at the Andrew Johnson National Historic Site, Greeneville, Tennessee.
Above: The Andrew Johnson house.
Right: Marker over Johnson's grave.
Below: The homestead of Andrew Johnson.

Johnson served a tempestuous term as president. He was impeached, but the Senate failed to convict him. Johnson was unable to carry out most of the moderate policies of Lincoln because of opposition and hatred on all sides. He lived to be elected once more to the Senate, in 1875. By this time some of the old hates were forgotten, and the former president received an ovation when he returned to the Senate floor.

In July of that same year, Andrew Johnson died. He was visiting his daughter, Mrs. Daniel Stover, near Elizabethton.

James K. Polk moved with his parents to Middle Tennessee when he was eleven years old. He began his law career in Columbia, then served Tennessee as state legislator. He was elected to the U.S. Congress where he was Speaker of the House from 1835 to 1839, and he served as governor from 1839 to 1841.

In 1844 the Democratic party picked Polk as their candidate; he defeated Henry Clay. It has been said that few other presidents ever accomplished as many of their presidential objectives as Polk.

James K. Polk died in Nashville in 1849; he and his wife are buried in a tomb on the state capitol grounds.

TWO FOR TEXAS

When he was about sixteen, Sam Houston ran away from his parents' farm and was adopted by Chief Olooteka on Hiwassee Island, near Dayton. He lived with the Indians for three years and came to know their ways—some say better than any other non-Indian. In later years he represented the Cherokee in Washington and worked hard for their interests.

Houston taught in a one-room school near Maryville. Of teaching he once said,"I experienced a higher feeling of dignity and self-satisfaction [from teaching] than from any office or honor which I have since held." He did indeed hold offices of honor. In fact, he probably served in more high offices than any other man in United States history—congressman from Tennessee, governor of Tennessee, governor of Texas, commander-in-chief of the Texas army, president of the Republic of Texas, and United States senator from Texas.

A crisis in his career occurred when Houston was governor of Tennessee. His wife left him—no one knows why—and Houston resigned the governorship. An observer remarked, "He rose like a rocket, fell like a stick." Houston returned to his friends the Cherokee and lived with them for some time; finally he was able to overcome his personal problems and continue his remarkable career.

While Texas brought new life to Houston, it brought a hero's death to another Tennessean, Davy Crockett. Born in 1786 in a log cabin on the banks of the Nolichucky River, near Limestone, Crockett is one of America's most famous frontiersmen. His unique career took him from bear hunting on the frontier, to a hero's rank in the Creek Indian war, the state legislature, the United States Congress, and finally to martyrdom in the cause of Texas.

Crockett served in Congress for two terms. There his exaggerated backwoods dress, coonskin cap, and rustic humor attracted great attention. He opposed some of Jackson's policies and did not win

This modern-day "frontiersman" is a reminder of Tennessee's Davy Crockett, one of America's most famous frontiersman.

reelection. When he learned of his defeat, Crockett announced to his opponent, "You can go to hell, I'm going to Texas." He had been there less than two years when he became one of the six survivors of the Battle of the Alamo. But Crockett was shot by order of Mexican leader Santa Anna on March 6, 1836.

Davy Crockett wrote several books about his adventures. With his rifle, Old Betsy, he ranged from Hangover Mountain to Reelfoot Lake. Probably no one ever knew Tennessee better. Crockett told of one cold night when he had to climb up and down a tree all night to keep from freezing. He also told of being trapped in a hollow tree trunk; he grabbed the tail of a mother bear and jabbed her with his knife until she pulled him out.

These and many other adventures, a large number of them fictional, have made Davy Crockett's name one of the best known of the frontier.

OTHERS IN THE PUBLIC EYE

One of the better known American statesmen of recent years was Cordell Hull, who was born near Byrdstown and became one of the most prominent secretaries of state. He served in the House of Representatives, then in the Senate, from which he resigned to become secretary of state under Franklin D. Roosevelt in 1933. He served in that post until 1944—longer than any other person in history. In 1945 he was awarded the Nobel Peace Prize.

Another cabinet member from Tennessee was John Bell, who served as secretary of war under William H. Harrison. He had been a United States senator and ran for president in 1860 on the Constitutional party ballot.

Peter Staub was a consul from Switzerland in the United States. After becoming a United States citizen, he served as an American consul in Switzerland. Among other accomplishments, he built Staub's Theater in Knoxville.

One of the most brilliant generals of the Civil War was Nathan Bedford Forrest, born at Chapel Hill, Tennessee, in 1821. He started as a private in the Confederate army and rose to high rank through ability and daring. He became known as the Wizard of the Saddle, making many legendary attacks along the border states.

A hero of earlier conflicts was General James Winchester of Castalian Springs. He was a prominent military leader of the Revolution and the War of 1812, as well as a renowned Indian fighter. He also was one of the founders of Memphis.

Another military leader of distinction was David Glasgow Farragut, born in a log cabin at Lowe's Ferry, on the Tennessee River. He was the first man to hold the rank of admiral in the American navy. His greatest victories were the capture of New Orleans and, later, the capture of Mobile during the Civil War.

A distinguished member of a prominent black family was J.C. Napier, grandson of the founder of Napier Iron Works. During his more than ninety years of life, he was an attorney, banker, and member of the Nashville School Board. President Taft appointed him register of the United States Treasury. A school, park, and court all bear his name in Memphis.

Other prominent black political leaders include R.R. (Bob) Church of Memphis and Samuel A. McElwee, who won a seat in the state legislature while still a student at Fisk University.

One of the leading physicians of the South was Dr. Robert Felton Boyd. He founded Mercy Hospital, Nashville's first for blacks. Another leading black physician was Dr. F.A. Stewart, a graduate of Harvard Medical School.

Among inventors, few have had more impact than the Rust brothers, John D. and Mack D. of Memphis, who developed the mechanical cotton picker. Dr. Charles Herty of Daisy and David Hughes of Springfield improved the telegraph.

CREATIVE TENNESSEANS

Few adventure writers had a larger following than Richard Halliburton of Memphis. He planned unusual stunts in romantic and faraway places and then wrote appealing accounts of his adventures.

Statue in Memphis honors W.C. Handy, the father of the blues and composer of the "St. Louis Blues," "Beale Street Blues," and "Memphis Blues."

Other prominent Tennessee literary figures include Opie Read and George Washington Harris, humorists; Thomas Hughes, author of *Tom Brown's School Days;* poet Allen Tate; James Weldon Johnson, black poet and scholar; and Adolph S. Ochs, Chattanooga newspaperman.

W.C. Handy can be credited with creating a whole new vocabulary of musical expression and influencing an entire segment of the musical population. Handy, the Memphis composer of the "St. Louis Blues," "Beale Street Blues," and "Memphis Blues," is generally recognized as the originator of the blues.

In an entirely different field of music, John Wesley Work was the author of *Folk Songs of the American Negro,* the first serious study of black American music.

William Edward West is called the first artist in Tennessee. He gained prominence in Europe as a portrait painter. Artist Washington Cooper of Nashville became known as the Man of a Thousand Portraits. Carey Orr and Joe Parrish gained reputations as leading cartoonists of their times.

Perhaps the most highly regarded artist of Tennessee is George De Forest Brush, whose work hangs in leading museums, including New York's Metropolitan. William Edmundson began his career as a carver of tombstones and went on to become one of the country's leading black sculptors.

SUCH INTERESTING PEOPLE

"If I had a thousand lives, I would lose them all here before I would betray my friend or the confidence of my informer," declared nineteen-year-old Sam Davis. He then turned slowly, mounted the scaffold, and dropped to his death.

Davis, one of Tennessee's most notable heroes, was captured by Federal troops while carrying military information about the North hidden in his boot. Union General G.M. Dodge tried to make him reveal the source of his information, but Davis refused. "Let come what must, I keep my trust," he is quoted as saying. Sentenced to death, Sam Davis rode to the scaffold on his coffin.

A hero of the Battle of Horseshoe Bend in the Creek War was John Williams, who served under Andrew Jackson. After this battle, Jackson is supposed to have declared,"Williams, you have this day made me famous!"

A hero of many wars was John Lusk, who fought in the siege of Quebec. He was present when Wolfe was killed on the Plains of Abraham, served under Benedict Arnold in his campaign into Canada, took part in the battle of Saratoga, and fought in the campaigns in which both Burgoyne and Cornwallis surrendered. Later he fought with General "Mad Anthony" Wayne in his Indian campaigns. Lusk lived to be 104 and died quietly in his bed at McMinnville in 1838.

A Tennessee heroine was Antoinette Polk, member of the prominent family that included Bishop Leonidas Polk. Antoinette overheard Union plans to capture a Confederate force. Hurrying off on her horse to warn the Southerners, she was pursued by Union men, who succeeded only in capturing a plume from her hat. In later years Antoinette Polk married the Baron de Charette and went abroad to live.

Another Tennessee woman loyal to the Confederate cause was Caroline Meriwether Goodlet, who founded the United Daughters of the Confederacy. She and her sister, newspaper columnist Dorothy Dix, were born near Bethlehem.

Del Rio was the birthplace of one of the best-known women singers of our history. Soprano Grace Moore became known through her work in opera and motion pictures.

A young truck driver named Elvis Presley walked down a Memphis street one day in 1954. He turned into the Sun Record Company's do-it-yourself studio and paid three dollars to make a record for his mother. Elvis became one of the most famous performers in the history of rock music. He died suddenly, at the age of 42, in 1977. He was a multimillionaire.

Memphis has high regard for another entertainer, television star Danny Thomas, who tirelessly raised funds for the St. Jude Hospital.

In sports, dentist Cary Middlecoff of Memphis became one of the most prominent golfers of his day.

Teaching and Learning

Tennessee has an unusual number of colleges and universities. Nashville has long been known as a center of education.

Higher education in Tennessee had its beginnings in 1794, when the Reverend Hezekiah Balch's school received its charter. In the same year Blount College was founded at Knoxville. It took its name from the territorial governor. Barbara Blount, daughter of the governor, was among the first students. Blount College was succeeded by East Tennessee College, which became East Tennessee University, and finally, in 1879, the University of Tennessee.

The university began as a coeducational school; but soon women were barred, and it remained segregated until 1893.

One of the best-known institutions of its kind is the George Peabody College for Teachers. Peabody usually is ranked as one of the top three American colleges for teacher training.

Another well-known Nashville institution is Vanderbilt University, chartered in 1872 under the name of the Central University of the Methodist Episcopal Church, South. Wealthy railroad magnate Cornelius Vanderbilt gave it a large endowment, and it took his name in 1873. Since that time it has received much larger grants from the Carnegie and Rockefeller foundations. Vanderbilt has long been considered one of the leading institutions of the South.

In 1866 Fisk University was founded to provide higher education for blacks. Over the years it has been one of the foremost influences in black education. Associated with Fisk is Meharry Medical College, an institution that has trained many outstanding medical men and women.

George L. White, treasurer of Fisk University, organized a choral group in 1867 to raise funds for the university through concerts. By 1871 the Fisk Jubilee Singers were good enough to tour Europe. The group was received with great enthusiasm and raised $150,000 — enough to buy the university campus and build Jubilee Hall. Over the years, the Fisk Jubilee Singers have become one of the best-known musical groups anywhere.

Other four-year Nashville colleges include Belmont, David

66

Lipscomb, Scarritt College for Christian Workers, Tennessee State University, and Trevecca Nazarene College.

Among Memphis colleges are Southwestern at Memphis, Memphis State University, Christian Brothers College, LeMoyne-Owen, and the Memphis Academy of Arts.

The University of the South at Sewanee, generally known as Sewanee University, was begun by the Protestant Episcopal church in 1857. It is especially known for its *Sewanee Review,* the oldest literary quarterly magazine continuously published in this country.

Private schools and academies were required to carry most of the load of education in Tennessee until Andrew Johnson became governor. When he addressed the legislature in 1853, he said: "At the present period, and for a long time past, our common schools have been doing little or no good, but on the contrary have been rather in the way than otherwise. There is one way that the children of the state can be educated . . . and that is to levy and collect a tax from the people of the whole state."

Although opposed by many, Johnson pushed through laws that set up standard examinations for teachers, permitted women to be employed as teachers, and provided money for the schools through a property tax. This was the beginning of effective public education in the state.

Enchantment of Tennessee

"Tennessee is a land of superlatives," according to former Governor Frank G. Clement. "It contains large areas where the curious, unusual, and scientific combine with the primitive."

ATHENS OF THE SOUTH: NASHVILLE

Nashville must certainly be considered one of the most cosmopolitan cities of the United States, with a personality that is a combination of diverse factors. It has the world's only full-scale reproduction of the Parthenon at Athens; several religious publishing houses; more than six hundred churches, including several denominational headquarters; the second largest recording industry in the nation; the largest investment banking center in the South; a variety of industries; and the Grand Ole Opry.

In 1779 James Robertson, called the Father of Tennessee by Andrew Jackson, led a small band of pioneers into **Middle Tennessee**. The pioneers settled on the banks of the Cumberland River, and soon thirty flatboats reached the settlement, bearing additional settlers and supplies. Nearby was the trading post of Timothe De Monbreun, set up in a cave on the river bank. De Monbreun became one of the leading citizens of the new settlement.

The new community was named Fort Nashborough in honor of Francis Nash, a North Carolina general who was killed in the Revolutionary War. We know it today as Nashville. A part of old Fort Nashborough has been re-created and may still be seen in Nashville.

Much more imposing is the complex of state government buildings, surmounted by the capitol on the highest part of the hill.

The capitol is built on old Cedar Knob, part of a tract of land that once was traded, along with a rifle, to pay off the balance owed on a

Opposite: Nashville's reproduction of the Parthenon at Athens

*The state capitol,
in Nashville, was
completed in 1855
and was completely
overhauled and
remodeled in 1953.*

cow. About thirty years later the city bought the site from the former owner of the cow, Judge George W. Campbell, for thirty thousand dollars.

The building's cornerstone was laid in 1845, and it was completed in 1855. The capitol architect, William Strickland, who died in 1854, was buried in a vault built into the walls of the building. In 1953 the capitol was given a complete overhaul and remodeling.

Inside the building are busts and plaques honoring the Taylor brother-governors, Alfred and Robert Love, Mark R. Cockrill, William Haskell Neal, Marion Dorset, Matthew F. Maury, George Washington, Albert Gleaves, Andrew Jackson, David G. Farragut, and others.

For the Tennessee Centennial Exposition of 1897, a full-scale reproduction of the Parthenon at Athens was built at Nashville of temporary materials. The people of Nashville were so taken with the replica that they had it rebuilt of more permanent material.

An even more famous building is the Hermitage, home of Andrew Jackson. Now a national historic landmark, the building was preserved largely through the work of the Ladies Hermitage Association. In the garden the frontiersman, soldier, president, and statesman lies buried beside his beloved Rachel.

Another prominent estate near Nashville is Belle Meade, one of the most famous horse-breeding farms of the United States. It is said to be the first place in America to have bred thoroughbred horses. A part of the Battle of Nashville was fought on the front lawn during the Civil War. Dunham Station log cabin, on the grounds, was used as a stopping place on the Old Natchez Trace.

The Nashville skyline

Travelers Rest is now a historical museum.

Travelers Rest is another old house now used as a historical museum, with period furniture and the reconstructed offices of Judge John Overton. It also contains Indian relics and slave cabins.

Other museums include the Tennessee State Museum in the War Memorial Building, the Children's Museum of Art, History and Science, the Fine Arts Center at Tennessee Botanical Gardens, and the Country and Western Music Museum.

The boom in country and western music is headquartered in Nashville. Musicians claim that there truly is a "Nashville sound." Only New York City outranks Nashville in the recording industry, and music in the city is a multimillion dollar business.

Opryland U.S.A., near Nashville, is an entertainment park and home of the Grand Ole Opry House.

OTHER MIDDLE TENNESSEE POINTS OF INTEREST

One of the most interesting homes in Middle Tennessee is Oaklands at Murfreesboro, a center of social life before the Civil War. Murfreesboro was once the capital of Tennessee but a fire destroyed the courthouse, so the legislature met at Nashville and never returned to Murfreesboro.

Near Murfreesboro is Stones River National Military Park and Cemetery, scene of some of the bloodiest fighting of the Civil War. In the park is a monument believed to be the first Civil War memorial.

Not far from Lawrenceburg is Davy Crockett Birthplace State Park. Another trailblazer is remembered in the Meriwether Lewis Monument near Hohenwald; the site where the explorer met his mysterious death is now a national monument.

The Tennessee Walking Horse National Celebration at Shelbyville is one of the greatest horse shows in the world. Each year a new world's champion is selected, and thousands of dollars in prizes are awarded.

James K. Polk's father's home at Columbia is now a national historic landmark. Another is the Carter House near Franklin. It serves as a memorial to the Battle of Franklin.

Two other interesting homes are Tulip Grove, near Lebanon, and the Cragfront mansion, near Gallatin. Tulip Grove was the home of Andrew Jackson Donelson, nephew of the president. Jackson built it to patch up a quarrel with his nephew Donelson. Cragfront was built

Each August the Tennessee Walking Horse (left) is honored at the Tennessee Walking Horse National Celebration in Shelbyville.

The Memphis skyline at sunset.

in 1798 by General James Winchester, who brought carpenters 700 miles (1120 kilometers) through the wilderness to quarry the stone from nearby bluffs and hand-hew the wood from the dense Tennessee forests.

Near Pikeville is Fall Creek Falls State Park and Forest. The falls is said to be the highest in the eastern United States. Another natural attraction is the beautiful Sequatchie Valley, near Crossville.

MEMPHIS

Memphis was laid out in 1819 by Andrew Jackson and two partners Because the land grant from North Carolina was somewhat questionable, Jackson soon withdrew. He named the city after old Memphis on the Nile in Egypt; both cities were on the greatest rivers of their continents. The name is supposed to mean "place of good abode."

74

After an epidemic of yellow fever in 1878, the city surrendered its charter and was put under direct state control until 1893. Today, however, the city enjoys great prosperity. The hub of a three-state area, Memphis is known as the Chicago of the South. There are hundreds of industries. It is the largest cotton market in the world, and a third of the entire cotton crop of the country is sold through Memphis. Memphis also is the world's largest producer of cottonseed products and ranks first in the world as a hardwood lumber market and producer of hardwood flooring.

The Defense Depot is a city within a city. It has ninety buildings on 642 acres (257 hectares). The Defense Industrial Plant Equipment Center is the centralized managing point for industrial plant equipment for the entire Defense Department.

Memphis pioneered in two popular food fields. Clarence Saunders was the first to introduce the self-service grocery, and Memphis claims the world's first drive-in restaurant.

The city has won four awards as the nation's cleanest city; it also has been cited as the safest city and the quietest city; unnecessary horn honking brings a fine. Memphis takes pride in having the largest medical center of the South.

Memphis's civic center is a major attraction. So is Chucalissa, a prehistoric town. Ten houses and a temple have been uncovered and rebuilt.

Clarence Saunders's palatial home has become a Memphis museum, popularly known as the Pink Palace. In addition to natural history collections and art objects, it includes a planetarium and houses the Memphis Little Theater.

One of the best-known houses in the region, Magevney Home, is open to the public. Another shrine of a different type is Graceland, home of the late Elvis Presley. Thousands visit the site each year.

Exciting events and activities of the city include Mississippi River excursions on the *Memphis Queen II,* productions of the Memphis Showboat, the largest rodeo east of the Mississippi, the national bird dog championships, and the Cotton Carnival.

Rivaling the Mardi Gras celebration in New Orleans, the Cotton Carnival opens each May with a colorful river pageant featuring the arrival of the King and Queen of Cotton on river boats at the Memphis dock. Parades with extravagant floats, dances, tours of antebellum homes, a children's festival, band concerts, a downtown midway, special art exhibits, a sailing regatta, and the grand coronation of the king and queen are highlights of the Memphis gala.

THE REST OF THE WEST

An event of unusual interest to sportsmen is the annual National Field Trials for Bird Dogs, held at Grand Junction. This is to the

The Pink Palace in Memphis, once
a palatial home, is now a museum.

sporting dog world what the World Series is to baseball. Dogs that have won local honors come from all over the country to compete for the national championships.

The clamor of the field trials contrasts with the quiet of Shiloh National Military Park, where one of the nation's fiercest battles was fought. Shiloh was the site of the first battlefield tent hospital ever set up to treat the wounded. A visitor center near Pittsburg Landing shows relics, maps, and films relating to the battle.

Jackson recalls two almost legendary figures who were both real enough in life. John A. Murrell, who lived a double life as a preacher-bandit, carried on a life of crime that would have made gangster John Dillinger seem tame. From his headquarters near Jackson, Murrell directed the activities of robbers and murderers who operated throughout several states. Much of their loot was stored in a fortresslike stronghold in Arkansas on the Mississippi River.

Murrell created a formal organization known as the Mystic Brotherhood of Criminals. Many consider it the model for the Ku Klux Klan. At length Murrell was caught and served ten years in prison. His organization disintegrated while he was in jail.

Jackson's other notable character was a great contrast. Railroader John Luther Jones was one of the best-known engineers on the Illinois Central line. He was famous for his ability to use the locomotive's steam whistle: "And the switchmen they knew by the engine's moans, that the man at the throttle was Old Casey Jones." He was also renowned for always being on time. One day he took the throttle of the Cannon Ball Express, substituting for a sick friend. The express was late; Casey was making up time when he crashed into a freight train that could not get out of the way fast enough. Casey Jones was killed. A friend and admirer, Wallace Sunders, an engine wiper, made up a ballad about Casey and his death. Casey Jones has become one of the romantic figures in the folklore of railroading.

Today Casey's home is owned by the city of Jackson and maintained as a railroad museum. Of special interest is a real steam locomotive, an exact duplicate of the one Casey Jones rode to his death.

One of the country's most unusual lakes—born in an earthquake—occupies part of the northwest corner of Tennessee. One of the most brutal episodes in Reelfoot Lake's history occurred in 1908. A group of promoters drew up plans to drain the lake, leaving the rich, fertile land of the lake bottom for farming. Lake fishermen banded together and one night lynched one of the promoters. This murder may have saved one of the country's natural wonders. The lake still provides fishing and recreation for thousands of visitors. Its banks are lined with statuesque cypress trees. In season, waterfowl are everywhere, and it has one of the most abundant fish populations in the world.

Another lake recreation area is the Land between the Lakes region, in the country between the Tennessee and Cumberland rivers.

Fort Donelson National Military Park and Cemetery, near Dover, is the scene of one of the early battles of the Civil War. The site contains the fort, said to be the best preserved of all Civil War forts. Here are the earthworks, rifle pits, and water batteries, and the house where the surrender was taken.

Other military memories are preserved in Nathan Bedford Forrest Memorial Park, near Camden, overlooking the site where Forrest's cavalrymen destroyed a Union navy. The Forrest monument is built on Pilot Knob, highest point in western Tennessee.

One of the strangest of Tennessee stories concerns a wealthy man called John Davis Howard, who came to live in Denver, near Waverly, with his wife and son. He bought a farm and soon took a leading part in community affairs. At local fairs he liked to show off his skill with a revolver. Suddenly he disappeared, and it was not until Jesse James was killed that the people of Denver realized their neighbor was that famous outlaw.

CHATTANOOGA

The Tennessee River makes a great, seven-mile (eleven-kilometer) curve near the Georgia border; because the shape of the

*High Falls
at Rock City Gardens,
Lookout Mountain*

curve resembles a foot, it is called Moccasin Bend. Across the river, dominating the whole region, is a great ridge known by the Indians as *Tsatanugi,* meaning, "rock coming to a point." This is the northern end of the vast bulk of Lookout Mountain.

At this spot has grown one of Tennessee's leading cities, Chattanooga. The city had its start in the trading post of Cherokee Chief John Ross. Beginning in 1838, Ross' Landing was transformed into Chattanooga, now a diversified city of many industries, where Coca-Cola in bottles was born and where miniature golf had its inception.

The attractions of the city include the George Thomas Hunter Gallery of Art, and the Anna Safley Houston Memorial Antique Museum. The John Ross home has been restored and may be seen much as it was in the days of the city's founding. The Siskin Memorial Foundation has a museum of religious and ceremonial art.

Mighty Lookout Mountain has many points of interest. Its almost flat top, towering to 2,391 feet (3,826 kilometers), extends many miles into Georgia and Alabama. One of the exciting ways to reach the top is by the Inclined Railroad, the steepest of its type in the world. One of the novel features of the mountain is a cave where Ruby Falls drops 145 feet (232 kilometers). One of the country's most widely advertised tourist attractions is Rock City Gardens, on the edge of the mountain, with many fine views and natural features. From here seven states can be seen on a fair day.

Many memories of the Battle above the Clouds are retained on Lookout Mountain, including the restored Cravens House, where much of the fighting took place, and Point Park, poised at the tip of the mountain. At the base of the mountain is the Confederama, in which thousands of miniature soldiers refight the Battle of Chattanooga in a motorized display.

Most of the Civil War battlefields of the area have been incorporated into Chickamauga and Chattanooga National Military Park, oldest and largest in the country. A large portion of the park lies outside the Tennessee state boundaries. The park contains major battle sites, including Lookout Mountain, Missionary Ridge, Signal Point on Signal Mountain, Orchard Knob in Chattanooga, and Chickamauga in Georgia.

Chickamauga Dam, almost a mile (1.6 kilometers) long, forms Chickamauga Lake, 34,500 acres (13,800 hectares) of water providing boating, docks, marina, fishing, swimming, and water skiing.

KNOXVILLE

Knoxville was settled in 1786 by Revolutionary War veterans and named for Henry Knox, secretary of war under George Washington. Today Knoxville is renowned as a trading center and headquarters of the Tennessee Valley Authority. It transformed its business district into a downtown shopping center called Market Square Mall, studied by city planners from all over the world.

Millions of tourists visit the city each year for its many attractions and because it is the gateway to the Smoky Mountains region.

One of the attractions is Governor William Blount's mansion, first frame house in the country west of the mountains. It once was the center of the military and social life of the whole region. It stands now as it did in the late 1700s and contains many items associated with its owner. Another restored historic building is Confederate Memorial Hall, maintained by the Daughters of the Confederacy as a memorial and museum.

On the campus of the University of Tennessee is the Frank H. McClung Museum, an outstanding building with changing art shows and exhibits of natural science and history. Another museum is the Dulin Gallery of Art, housed in a building designed by John Russell Pope, architect of the National Gallery of Art.

At nearby Oak Ridge is the first museum dedicated to atomic power—the American Museum of Atomic Energy. It is maintained by the Oak Ridge Institute of Nuclear Studies. There is a demonstration of the uses of atomic material, and of the way mechanical "hands" are used to handle radioactive material. One of the attractions is the model of an actual nuclear reactor.

The city of Oak Ridge is a child of the atom, built during World War II to house the hundreds who were shaping uranium 235 into the first atomic bombs. It once was one of the world's most secret places, but now thousands visit the area every year.

The Knoxville skyline

GATLINBURG AND THE SMOKIES

One of the most pleasant drives in America takes the visitor up the breathtaking canyon of the West Fork of the Little Pigeon River. Highway 441, which climbs this rugged canyon, is four lanes wide, and it provides marvelous vistas of the rugged mountains of the east—the Tennessee slope of Great Smoky Mountains National Park.

The canyon broadens slightly, and clinging to its side is one of America's most popular mountain resort communities—Gatlinburg. Only a few years ago there was only one hotel and a few houses in all of Gatlinburg. Today motels and tourist and convention attractions have spread up the mountainside and even hang out over the river.

Main Street is lined with shops and tourist attractions. In the beginning, the Gatlinburg shops sold almost exclusively the fine handmade crafts produced in the surrounding area. Many of the shops still offer these, and some of the craft items are made in the shops while visitors look on. The important revival of hand skills was sparked by Pi Beta Phi Settlement School at Gatlinburg, where experts taught the ancient skills. The first craft shop was the Arrowcraft.

The annual Craftsman Fair at Gatlinburg in October is probably the outstanding event of its kind in the country.

There are some who say that the commercial shops and restaurants and the increasing number of motels, which now accommodate thousands nightly, have ruined the quaint and primitive atmosphere of the early Gatlinburg.

However, in its place has mushroomed a community unlike any other. In season, the streets are more crowded than Fifth Avenue or State Street. The Smoky Sky Lift carries a stream of visitors up Crockett Mountain; the convention center is booked solid. But only three or four minutes away are quiet valleys, where no sound is heard except the rush of a stream or the shuffle of a stone dislodged by a squirrel, rabbit, or black bear.

Gatlinburg ends abruptly, and the Great Smoky Mountains National Park begins a few blocks out on Highway 441. A move to

Mt. Leconte, Great Smoky Mountain National Park

create a national park in the loftiest part of the Smokies was begun as early as 1899, but much of the park came into public hands only through the dedication of the Rockefeller family. The Great Smoky Mountains National Park Bill, signed into law by President Coolidge in 1926, preserves forever the place known to the Indians as the Land of a Thousand Smokes.

Most visitors simply go over the main highway, pass Newfound Gap, and go down the other side, or take the turn to Clingmans Dome to admire the vista from Tennessee's highest point—6,643 feet (2,025 meters). Those who stay longer may wander up the side roads and trails to view the giant trees in primeval forests, admire Laurel and other falls, ascend such scenic trails as Charlies' Bunyon, admire the greatest variety of wild flowers in the country, ski, or enjoy other sports in season.

Along the crest of the mountains that form the border between Tennessee and North Carolina winds the spectacular Appalachian Trail, a unique path for hikers, which ends in faraway Maine.

Those visitors who travel the side roads to Cades Cove or Greenbrier Cove are rewarded by tiny communities that still exist much as they did in pioneer times.

THE REST OF THE EAST

The tailor shop at Greeneville has been restored, along with the Andrew Johnson home, as Andrew Johnson National Historic Site. The brick building has furnishings and tools of the tailor craft with which Johnson supported his family while still in his early teens. Here he taught himself by hiring young men to read to him.

After Johnson's tragic years in the White House, he returned to Greeneville, where he was elected once again to the United States Senate, the only ex-president in history to be so elected.

Other attractions of East Tennessee include historic Fort Loudoun, reconstructed near Madisonville; Davy Crockett Birthplace Park, near Jonesboro; the Crockett Tavern and Museum, Morristown; Sam Houston Schoolhouse, Maryville; Norris Dam and Lake on the Clinch River; Cumberland Gap National Historical Park; and the annual ramp (wild onion) festival at Cosby.

The cities of northeastern Tennessee include Kingsport, Johnson City, Elizabethton, and Bristol.

Bristol is two towns, one in Tennessee, the other in Virginia— each with its own post office. State Street divides the two states.

Bristol is an important factory town, producing calculating machines, textiles, electronic items, and metal goods. It is also a major shopping center. Nearby is Bristol Caverns.

Kingsport was a small town until World War I. Then it grew into a city with many industries, including the huge Tennessee Eastman plant.

Chartered in 1917 as a model industrial community, Kingsport is one of the few cities in the world where an uncut log can arrive in town one day and be transformed into a finely bound book by the next. The wood is converted to paper on one side of Center Street, then ends up as a bound book at Kingsport Press on the other side of Center Street.

Johnson City is a principal auction point for burley tobacco, a center of railroad shops and marketing, and a shipping point for the cattle, eggs, and alfalfa of Washington County. Near Johnson City is Rocky Mount Historic Shrine, which informally served Territorial Governor William Blount as the first capitol west of the Allegheny Mountains while he waited for his own home and capitol to be built. Here the beginnings of organization came to the territory.

Restored, Rocky Mount now serves as a museum of the frontier. Other points of interest in the area are East Tennessee State University, Milligan College, Steed College of Technology, and three dams—Boone, Fort Patrick Henry, and Cherokee.

On the lawn of the county courthouse in Elizabethton is a monument that commemorates the Watauga Association, first informal government set up west of the mountains. In Elizabethton also was held the first court west of the Alleghenies.

Near Elizabethton, on the pollen-free top of Roan Mountain, grows a garden not planted by people. Here are 600 acres (240 hectares) of the rare purple rhododendron. When the plants are at the peak of their bloom—not every year—the entire mountaintop is covered with an expanse of blossoms unequaled anywhere else.

As visitors wander among the towering, waxy-leaved plants, covered with clusters of bright purple, they are apt to agree with the Tennessee supporter who exclaimed, "Everything about Tennessee these days is coming into full bloom!"

Spectacular Tennessee sunset

Handy Reference Section

Instant Facts

Became the 16th state, June 1, 1796
Capital—Nashville, settled 1779
Nickname—The Volunteer State
State motto—"Agriculture and Commerce"
State animal—Raccoon
State bird—Mockingbird
State tree—Tulip poplar
State flower—Iris
State stone—Agate
State song—"The Tennessee Waltz"
Area—42,244 square miles (109,411 square kilometers)
Rank in area—34th
Greatest length (north to south)—120 miles (193 kilometers)
Greatest width (east to west)—430 miles (692 kilometers)
Geographic center—Rutherford, 5 miles (8 kilometers) northeast of
        Murfreesboro
Highest point—6,643 feet (2,025 meters), Clingmans Dome
Lowest point—182 feet (55 meters)
Number of counties—95
Population—4,590,750 (1980 census)
Rank in population—17th
Population density—109 per square mile (42 per square kilometer),
        1980 census
Population center—In Rutherford County, 8 miles (12.8 kilometers) southwest of
        Murfreesboro
Birth rate—15.6 per 1,000 people
Infant mortality rate—21.8 per 1,000 births
Physicians per 100,000—130

Principal Cities—		
Memphis	646,356	(1980 census)
Nashville	455,651	
Knoxville	183,139	
Chattanooga	169,565	
Jackson	49,131	
Johnson City	39,753	

You Have a Date with History

1541—Hernando De Soto probably visited the Memphis region
1673—Marquette and Jolliet come to West Tennessee; Needham and Arthur
    explore the east

1682—Sieur de La Salle constructs Fort Prudhomme
1714—French trader Charleville begins trading post on site of present Nashville
1730—Sir Alexander Cuming makes friends with Cherokee
1736—Sieur de Bienville defeated by Chickasaw
1757—Fort Loudon completed
1760—Cherokee capture Fort Loudon
1769—First cabin built on Watauga River
1772—Watauga Association organized
1779—Jonesboro laid out; first formally established town
1780—Nashville established
1784—State of Franklin organized
1786—Knoxville settled
1790—United States accepts cession of Tennessee from North Carolina
1794—Cherokee power broken
1796—Statehood
1809—Meriwether Lewis dies in Tennessee
1811—Earthquake forms Reelfoot Lake
1819—Memphis laid out
1838—Chattanooga founded; Cherokee forced from Tennessee
1843—Nashville becomes permanent state capital
1846—30,000 volunteer for Mexican War, giving state its Volunteer State nickname
1855—Capitol building completed
1861—Secession
1862—Grant takes Forts Henry and Donelson; battles of Memphis and Shiloh
1863—Battles of Stones River, Chattanooga, Lookout Mountain
1864—Forrest destroys Johnsonville; Battles of Franklin, Nashville
1865—People vote to free slaves
1866—Tennessee readmitted to Union
1873—Cholera epidemic strikes Nashville
1878—5,000 dead of yellow fever at Memphis
1886—''War of the Roses''
1897—Centennial Exposition at Nashville
1908—Former Senator Carmack slain
1917—World War I begins in which 91,180 see service, 3,400 killed
1918—Alvin York becomes greatest hero of World War I
1920—Tennessee becomes deciding state to vote for 19th Amendment, providing women's suffrage
1925—Scopes trial
1926—Great Smoky Mountains National Park established
1933—Norris Dam begun
1937—Great Mississippi River flood
1941—World War II begins in which 315,501 see service, 7,727 killed
1963—Memphis airport opened
1966—Revenue from tourists reaches nearly $360,000,000.

1968—Assassination of Dr. Martin Luther King, Jr., at Memphis
1977—King assassin, James Earl Ray, recaptured after prison escape
1977—Elvis Presley dies
1982—World's Fair is held in Knoxville

Thinkers, Doers, Fighters

Bell, John
Brush, George De Forest
Crockett, David (Davy)
Farragut, David Glasgow
Forrest, Nathan Bedford
Halliburton, Richard
Handy, W.C.
Houston, Samuel (Sam)
Hull, Cordell
Jackson, Andrew
Johnson, Andrew
Jones, John Luther (Casey)
King, Dr. Martin Luther, Jr.
Middlecoff, Cary
Moore, Grace
Polk, James K.
Presley, Elvis
Read, Opie
Ross, John (Chief)
York, Alvin

Annual Events

February—Grand National Field Trials, Grand Junction
March—Southeastern 500 (Auto Race), Bristol
April—Ramp Festival, Cosby
April—Spring Wild flower Pilgrimage, Gatlinburg
April—Carter County Wild flower Tour, Elizabethton
April-May—Dogwood Arts Festival, Knoxville
April-May—Fish Fry, Paris
May—Strawberry Festival, Humboldt
May—East Tennessee Strawberry Festival, Dayton
May—Iroquois Steeplechase, Nashville
May—Cotton Carnival, Memphis
June—Roan Mountain Rhododendron Festival, Elizabethton
July—National Hillbilly Homecoming, Maryville
July—Volunteer 500 (Auto Race), Bristol
July-August—National Catfish Derby, Savannah
August—Cotton Ball, Chattanooga
August-September—Tennessee Walking Horse National Celebration, Shelbyville
September—Tri-State Fair, Chattanooga
September—Tennessee State Fair, Nashville
September—Naturalist Rally, Elizabethton
September-October—Mid-South Fair and Exposition, Memphis
October—One Gallus Fox Hunt and Bench Show, Eagleville
October—Fox Hound Field Trials and Bench Show, Cedars of Lebanon State Park
October—Craftsman's Fair, Gatlinburg

Governors of Tennessee

William Blount (Territorial Governor), 1790-1796
John Sevier 1796-1801
Archibald Roane 1801-1803
John Sevier 1803-1809
Willie Blount 1809-1815
Joseph McMinn 1815-1821
William Carroll 1821-1827
Sam Houston 1827-1829
William Hall 1829
William Carroll 1829-1835
Newton Cannon 1835-1839
James K. Polk 1839-1841
James C. Jones 1841-1845
Aaron V. Brown 1845-1847
Neill S. Brown 1847-1849
William Trousdale 1849-1851
William B. Campbell 1851-1853
Andrew Johnson 1853-1857
Isham G. Harris 1857-1862
Andrew Johnson 1862-1865
William G. Brownlow 1865-1869
DeWitt Clinton Senter 1869-1871
John C. Brown 1871-1875
James D. Porter 1875-1879
Albert S. Marks 1879-1881
Alvin Hawkins 1881-1883

William B. Bate 1883-1887
Robert Love Taylor 1887-1891
John P. Buchanan 1891-1893
Peter Turney 1893-1897
Robert Love Taylor 1897-1899
Benton McMillin 1899-1903
James B. Frazier 1903-1905
John I. Cox 1905-1907
Malcolm R. Patterson 1907-1911
Ben W. Hooper 1911-1915
Tom C. Rye 1915-1919
A.H. Roberts 1919-1921
Alfred A. Taylor 1921-1923
Austin Peay 1923-1927
Henry H. Horton 1927-1933
Hill McAlister 1933-1937
Gordon Browning 1937-1939
Prentice Cooper 1939-1945
Jim McCord 1945-1949
Gordon Browning 1949-1953
Frank G. Clement 1953-1959
Buford Ellington 1959-1963
Frank G. Clement 1963-1967
Buford Ellington 1967-1971
Winfield Dunn 1971-1975
Leonard Ray Blanton 1975-1979
Lamar Alexander 1979-

Index

91

92

94

ABOUT THE AUTHOR

With the publication of his first book for school use when he was twenty, **Allan Carpenter** began a career as an author that has spanned more than 135 books. After teaching in the public schools of Des Moines, Mr. Carpenter began his career as an educational publisher at the age of twenty-one when he founded the magazine *Teachers Digest*. In the field of educational periodicals, he was responsible for many innovations. During his many years in publishing, he has perfected a highly organized approach to handling large volumes of factual material: after extensive traveling and having collected all possible materials, he systematically reviews and organizes everything. From his apartment high in Chicago's John Hancock Building, Allan recalls, "My collection and assimilation of materials on the states and countries began before the publication of my first book." Allan is the founder of Carpenter Publishing House and of Infordata International, Inc., publishers of *Issues in Education* and *Index to U. S. Government Periodicals*. When he is not writing or traveling, his principal avocation is music. He has been the principal bassist of many symphonies, and he managed the country's leading non-professional symphony for twenty-five years.